# THE DISCIPLE'S TEXTBOOK

## ROBERT BAUER

*The Disciple's Textbook*

Trilogy Christian Publishers A Wholly Owned Subsidary of Trinity Broadcasting Network

2442 Michelle Drive Tustin, CA 92780

Copyright © 2022 by Robert Bauer

rights reserved. Printed in the USA.

Rights Department, 2442 Michelle Drive, Tustin, CA 92780.

Trilogy Christian Publishing/TBN and colophon are trademarks of Trinity Broadcasting Network.

Cover design by: Kristy Swank

For information about special discounts for bulk purchases, please contact Trilogy Christian Publishing.

Trilogy Disclaimer: The views and content expressed in this book are those of the author and may not necessarily reflect the views and doctrine of Trilogy Christian Publishing or the Trinity Broadcasting Network.

Manufactured in the United States of America

10 9 8 7 6 5 4 3 2 1

Library of Congress Cataloging-in-Publication Data is available.

ISBN: 979-8-88738-175-6

E-ISBN: 979-8-88738-176-3

# TABLE OF CONTENTS

# Chapter 1

## My Testimony

## Struggles with God and Scripture

Growing up, I was told, "You can be anything you want to be when you grow up." I saw both my parents working two jobs. I watched them grow their wealth with hard work and smart financial discipline. They taught my younger brother and me by their example.

We grew up in the suburbs around Detroit, Michigan. It was the late 1970s and early 1980s. We had seen the impact of imported cars and imported steel. Many people were leaving the area. They were following their jobs. I remember seeing bumper stickers that read, "Will the last person out of Michigan please shut off the lights."

It was hard for a high school graduate to find any job in 1984. Minimum wage was $3.35 an hour. I had a job making $3.65 an hour. I knew I wanted better for myself. My parents encouraged me. I tried a summer semester at the local community college. That didn't inspire me. I joined the United States Marine Corps. In the Marines, I was injured during active-duty training and obtained an honorable discharge under medical conditions. I am a disabled American veteran.

I was trying to make my life in Southern California in the late 1980s and early 1990s. I was engaged to a woman I was really in love with. We were struggling with making enough money to have the things every person should enjoy. Then she became pregnant.

I was excited. I knew it would be tough, but I foresaw us finally tying the knot and starting our family. Then she told me she didn't want to have the baby. I was very confused! I lobbied hard to follow through with our wedding plans and start our family. She not only did not want the child, but she no longer wanted to marry me!

That was not the worst part of it for me. My fiancé and her parents told me it was my responsibility to pay for half the abortion. I wanted the child; I wasn't considering abortion a possibility.

They told me, "You can't afford to take care of yourself. How are you going to afford a child?"

I answered, "Easier than paying for an abortion."

That sparked a fierce fight. It was the mother's choice. It was her body. If I was a better man, I could provide for a wife and a child. Since I couldn't afford to give a wife and a child a good life, I was not worthy of either.

I replied, "Killing an innocent life won't fix it either."

Suddenly everybody but me in that argument thought I had a mental problem. I was strenuously urged to go get psychiatric help. *Maybe they had some medicine that would balance me out.*

I absolutely refused to even go see a psychiatrist. I did not have a problem. I was not trying to murder an innocent life. The baby could be born and put up for adoption.

I refused to pay anything for the abortion. The money I contributed for rent, utilities, and groceries was diverted by them to pay for the abortion. I was very angry about that.

To add insult to injury, it was my job to take my fiancé to the clinic and wait for the *procedure* to be done and take her back to her parents. I was, of course, no longer welcome there.

On the way home from the clinic, my girl tells me about the jar they used to collect the aborted fetus. She said, "I couldn't see it really well, but I knew what it was."

I had horrible nightmares of my child trying to break out of a test tube after that.

To say the least, it put a huge strain on our relationship. We were suddenly back to boyfriend-girlfriend; she was at her parents, and she talked about seeing other people. I was renting a room from friends.

That is when I realized all the friends I had were her friends first. No matter what I did, those friends would lie for her and inform on me. Then came an important revelation, the date of her conception. I had to go back to the calendar and check the dates. We were in different states the whole week; she could have gotten pregnant.

By the time I figured it out and confronted her, she answered me with, "I have had three."

I guess that was to throw me off the offensive, but I was concerned, "If you keep doing that, when you really want one, you won't be able to have one."

She yelled at me, "Marylin Monroe had thirteen!"

I answered back, "Are you trying to set a record?"

It was a horrible situation and seemed so unfair. I had to get away from her, our relationship, and such careless disregard for human life.

I went to bar and started drinking. A friend of mine told me, "You are a great guy, but you have your priorities mixed up."

I know the friend was trying to encourage me through my difficult time, but it made me angry.

I had been raised Catholic. I was not practicing any religion at the time. I sure did blame God for what was going wrong, though. It was so bad for me that I took a pocket-size Bible and set it on fire. I let it burn while I listed for God all the things I believed He was allowing to hurt me. I told him I never asked to exist in the first place. I blamed Him for making me suffer unjustly.

After the Bible had burned more than halfway, I urinated on it to put out the fire. I told God, "That is what I think of Your Word." Then I went one step farther; I denied that there was any God. I couldn't stop there; I had to go to the next step too! I screamed at the universe, "I am god!" I kept up, "I am going to do things my way, and I don't care what the consequences are!"

If you have any amount of faith as you read the above, you know I just set myself up for a literal mountain of humiliation and suffering. If you have never really believed in any faith, you might read the above and say, "This guy finally figured it out."

The reason I publish this is, God uses broken vessels. I want all my readers to remember that as you continue to read this. I was very broken inside my heart and mind when I did these things. I said I was angry at God. Anger is a mask for other emotions. A big tough guy from Detroit, a Marine, he can't show weakness like pain or have emotions like shame and guilt; he has to be angry!

Instead of dealing with my pain, shame, and guilt, I blamed the world and made it my enemy. I was like a bull in a china shop recking everything good in my life. I convinced myself that if I drank enough, the pain wouldn't feel so bad. Then being too drunk made me sloppy. I needed a boost to keep me alert. I turned to methamphetamine. Now that gave me an edge like a buzz saw. I had to drink even more. That wasn't doing enough. I began to smoke marijuana in addition to drinking to offset the effects of the amphetamines.

I thought all the people who were doing the same thing were my friends. I ran around nightclubbing and barhopping. I did my day job and maintained a level of intoxication so I could complete my job functions satisfactorily. The lifestyle was addicting. Fear of missing out became a driving force. I would go seven days without sleep. When I did sleep, I slept for three days!

Through a series of unfortunate events and very poor decisions on my part, I lost everything. My job, my home, the vehicle I drove, and all the personal belongings I could not carry with me. None of my party friends were returning my calls. I was getting very hungry, losing weight. Think about that: I was not eating before, and now I had no intake, not even beer!

I was not done fighting yet. I was from Detroit; we never quit. I was a Marine, you could kill me, but you couldn't beat me. I was a belligerent young man with a chip on my shoulder as big as Mars. The god of war, Mars. Everything was a fight for me. I could see people deliberately change their path to avoid me when they saw me coming.

I remember trying to get a job at McDonald's so at least I could eat. The manager there turned me down, telling me he couldn't afford to pay a new employee for any hours worked. I was homeless. I showered at the beach and slept in buildings under construction. My alarm clock was the workers showing up and finding me squatting there. It got so bad I ended up with an infestation of tics!

To eat, I would collect cans and turn them in for enough money to buy a ramen noodle. I would walk into a business and use their hot water dispenser to make my ramen noodle. A lot of times, I was chased out of the building carrying all that I owned and trying not to spill my soup.

I borrowed money until I burned out all my family, relatives, and friends. I was on general assistance; then, I got sanctioned from general assistance because I missed an appointment. I was at the VA in Long Beach trying to get help as a disabled American veteran. The General Assistance Office made the appointment for me. They knew it was a scheduling conflict. I was there the day before, trying to get in early. They wouldn't see me. I didn't make it back on the day in question; I was on public transportation! The following day I was there when the doors opened. "Nope, not good enough; you get nothing, Mr. Bauer."

I thought that was my rock bottom. Guess I should have shut up at the point when I told God, "That is what I think of Your Word." I didn't stop my mouth back then; my troubles were not stopping now.

I literally prayed for God to take my life. I laid down to sleep and prayed I did not wake up. That doesn't work. I woke up the angriest I had ever been to that point in my life. I was starving to death a little more every day. I watched as thousands of people drove past in their luxury cars every day. I was walking, carrying all that I owned, my clothes saggy from losing so much weight. I felt that if there was some way for me to get back on my feet, I would do whatever it took. It didn't have to be legitimate business. I was desperate; this was my life in the balance.

I hustled and got a front on some marijuana. Of course, I couldn't sell it for what I paid for it, or should I say, what I promised to pay for it. I was in serious trouble with the dealer and thought I was going to be killed. Instead, I was given an opportunity to collect a few debts that other people owed—that would pay my debt.

I was knocking on a door in a low-income housing project. People coming and going everywhere. The door opened, and I pushed my way in. I simply said, "You know who you owe. It is time to pay. I am here to collect."

In this apartment were three little kids, all under five years old. A mom and a dad. The kids were in dirty diapers and/or clothes, filthy and obviously hungry. The dad was playing Mario Bros on Nintendo.

He barely noticed I was there. The mom, visibly pregnant, offered to have sex with me for the debt. I had to decline; I needed cash.

She laughed when she said, "We don't get our check until Friday." I remember thinking, *I don't have until Friday.*

Then an inspiration hit me. I walked over to the Nintendo counsel and ripped it out of the wall. I was on my way out of their apartment when I laughed and told them, "When you get what you owe, you can have this back."

It took them a couple of hours, but I had the debt money in cash. I returned the game system. Then I paid the dealer. The dealer was impressed. "How did you get cash from those people?"

I explained what I had done. Then I was offered a *better job* for the dealer. I thought I was doing good. I got my own apartment for the first time in months. I got medicine to relieve my tic infestation. I had the money to go grocery shopping again. I could buy new clothes. I could afford to do my laundry in a washer and drier instead of in the shower when I got one. I did what was asked of me. I didn't ask questions. I never made any demands.

Then came the day I was arrested! I knew better than to say anything. I took the heat for what I did. While I was in "state college," I reached out to my parents. They were not thrilled. I started to blame the whole world. It was dirty cops and crooked prosecutors; I had a dump truck public defender. It was people lying about what I did. Everybody was out to get me.

My mom asked me, "Are you a famous celebrity?"

I replied no.

She then asked me, "If no one knows you exist, how can everybody be out to get you?"

That was the first crack in my wall of denial. Other things began to show up in my life. I think it was getting clean. For the first time since my little Bible-burning party, I was sober for more than a day. It was very hard to deny all the evidence I left in my wake. Not even the Dream Team could get an acquittal for a guy who was seen by a dozen witnesses and caught on numerous security cameras.

As the realization, "It is not the whole world, it is me," began to set in, I had to reflect on where I went so wrong. I was raised well. Both my parents worked two jobs to give their children a life better than they had. I knew to obey the law. I had a decent work ethic. I was a high school graduate. A military veteran. I should have achieved a little bit more than I did.

Then came the realization of the amount of time I would have to serve and the age I would be when I finally paroled. I would still have no job, no home, no car, and nobody waiting for me. I had to get serious about living right if I didn't want to spend the rest of my life in a cage.

I guess I should have shut my mouth when I denied there was a God. I couldn't do that back then, and my troubles were not slowing down. Turns out in prison, there are a lot of gang members doing time. I had certainly rubbed some people the wrong way when I was out collecting for the connection. When word reached those people that I was doing time in such and such prison, they wanted payback. Someone came calling for blood!

I had a few fights in prison. I survived in no small part due to being from Detroit and a Marine. Now I was also a convicted felon doing hard times. It is a little too late to do the right thing now, or is it? I guess I should have shut my mouth when I claimed to be god myself. I didn't think I was going to make my parole date. If I didn't get myself killed, I would catch an institutional murder and be doing all day myself.

Then my brother wrote me. He was so proud. I was going to be an uncle! The realization shattered my battered wall of denial. My niece would be at least six years old before I could ever meet her. Guess I should have shut my mouth before I said, "I am going to do things my way, and I don't care what the consequences are!" I didn't stop myself back then, but things seemed to be about the worst I could imagine.

This was the point in 1994 that I caved in. Tough guy from Detroit, Marine, convicted felon, crying like a little baby in his prison cell, asking God to forgive him.

I asked God to forgive me for everything I could remember doing in my anger toward Him. I knew I had ruined my life. Becoming a *Bible thumper* or *Holy Roller* in prison was not highly esteemed inside the prison walls.

I told the other convicts I was there to do my time for me, and then I was paroling alone. I didn't get any prison tattoos; I didn't join any prison gangs. I programmed the way a model prisoner is supposed to. Prison is a tough place to get right with God. Other convicts want to test you. You are faced with many temptations. You see and hear things that are horrible. You are a victim of circumstance. The shot callers make the rules, and if you don't obey, you get hurt or killed.

It is a place where the tough and smart control the weaker and less intelligent. A lot of weak or afraid of confrontation prisoners get exploited in a multitude of ways. Child molesters and rapists are made to pay protection money. "Rats" and "snitches" usually have to lock up in protective custody if they make it that far. There are always those new prison guards who want to enforce every rule to the last letter of the law. They stir up drama and strife. Then there are the hard-core prisoners who do anything to slight the guards. At any time, a guy like me doing my time for myself can walk into a dangerous, potentially life-threatening incident. Just saying the wrong thing or not saying the right thing can cause a serious problem.

This is where my fear of God triumphed over all other fears. Here is where my doubts about God's supremacy in all ways dried up and blew away. Inside prison walls is where I learned that being distracted is a sure way to die. I saw many selfish people incarcerated and what that did to them. These four things, fear, doubt, distraction, and selfish pursuits, became the enemy of my faith. I had to fight them while doing my time and trying to learn Scripture.

The first time I took responsibility for my bad decisions and wrongful behavior was the first time I had the power to fix what was broken inside me. Blaming outside of me gave that power away. Who did the stinking thinking? I did. Whose heart was in the wrong place? Mine. Who committed the criminal acts? I did. Whose fault are my problems? Mine! Who can fix it? Only me. I had to get faith to get right with God and then fix all that was wrong in accordance with Scripture.

I did have the natural consequences for my actions to get through before I could practice my faith as a free man. I made myself a promise; no matter what it took, I was never going to let myself commit another crime.

I was able to study the Word from early in 1994 until my parole at the end of 1998. For over four years, I studied Scripture and applied what I learned in my life while serving my sentence. Prison is a vicious environment full of predators. Some of whom have no hope and nothing to lose.

There are, however, a few good convicts in prison. It was one such man that helped me understand Scripture more accurately and brought me so much closer to God spiritually. I called him a disciple of Scripture.

# Chapter 2

## A Benevolent Benefactor in a Dark Place

When I met this disciple of Scripture, he saw me in my misery and asked me one question, "Why are you so angry?"

I told him, "Because I have been arguing with God for a long time, and He does not fight fair."

My soon-to-be teacher of Scripture laughed at my answer. I was offended, "What is so funny about that?" I asked him.

He answered me, "If you don't know the rules, how can you say what is or is not fair?"

I answered, "He is supposed to be a God of love. Why does He make so many people suffer?"

My teacher answered me, "God doesn't make people suffer. He gave us all the knowledge of right and wrong and the free will to do anything we want. God just holds us accountable for our thoughts, words, and deeds. He allows us to experience the natural consequences of our deeds so we can learn from them."

I cannot tell you how angry that answer made me. I replied to him very coldly, "I didn't ask to exist! What is the point of living if I never had a chance to succeed in life?"

He replied, "Are you doing what you are because you know it is right or because you think it is what is expected of you?"

Now that question baffled me. I didn't know how to answer it. I wanted to say I was doing what I did because I knew it was right. The problem was, I wasn't sure what was right at that point in my life.

As my friendship with this disciple of Scripture grew, I learned that a lot of the things I believed were biblical turned out to be contrary to what Scripture said. Thus began a long process of reading the Bible for myself to know what it said and thus know right from wrong.

Can you imagine how proud of myself I was when I finished the whole Bible for the first time? I was reading a chapter out of the Old and New Testaments every day. It took a while. I finished many Bible studies during this time. I was in a Bible study group the whole time. I was digging into the Word, seeking the treasure it promised.

My teacher told me, "Read it again."

I thought I was done. It was an accomplishment. Nobody could take away what I learned. He smiled at me and asked, "How many times do you think I have read the entire Bible?"

"I have no idea," I answered.

He told me he was starting his fifteenth time reading the Bible.

I asked, "Why?"

He answered me, "Because every time I read it, I get something new from it."

This was coming from the man I had learned to respect as my mentor and teacher. Even though we were both in prison, I saw the better quality of time he was serving compared to a lot of other people there. I saw his devotion to helping people through the Lord and Scripture. Many people from every walk of life came to him with questions, and he just seemed to know the answer they needed. He was getting many letters from people on the outside asking him questions. He would answer them all. He had so many thank you cards from the real world that it was humbling. He said many times, "I love helping people."

At first, I started reading the Bible a second time with more than a little doubt I would get anything new out of it. I was stunned the first time I realized I got something new from a scripture I had already read. I began to read the Bible more and more. I made time for it in the morning with a cup of coffee. I read it before going to sleep. I had a Bible at work. Any time I had to read, I read the Bible. I was amazed at all the new things I discovered during my second reading of the Bible.

I knew that was a secret. I never thought of reading it more than once. I know better now. My teacher saw the growth in my walk. I was always asking more questions. He was always available to answer my questions from scripture. His devotion to God showed me what it meant to be a disciple of Scripture.

It was the greatest gift anyone has ever given me. I want to share this gift with anyone who will receive it. When I say things need to be done a certain way, it is not because I made up such rules; it is because that is how I learned to do it. I learned it from scripture. God's Word taught me. God's Word is what I am sharing. I have been blessed with a more accurate understanding of scripture as I continue to read the Bible every day. Now I am on my seventh time reading the Bible from cover to cover. Yes, I still learn new things almost every time I read from it.

# Chapter 3

## What is a Disciple of Scripture?

A disciple of Scripture is a person who has dedicated themselves to the understanding of God's Word. When our Lord and Savior walked this earth, He called His disciples from the people around Him. He said, "I am the way, the truth, and the life" (John 14:6, NKJV).

The word of God became the flesh incarnate in Jesus Christ (John 1:14).

For people today, it is impossible to be disciples of Jesus Christ. There is no physical person alive today who knew Jesus Christ when He walked this earth. The closest thing we have to the living Christ is the divinely inspired scripture. Making oneself a disciple of Scripture will bring us the closest we can possibly be to Christ.

"[...] blessed are those who have not seen and yet have believed" (John 20:29, NIV).

Unlike following a person and learning from them, a disciple of Scripture must teach themselves. They have to study the scriptures daily. They apply what the scripture teaches in everyday life. The lessons given to the chosen people by their prophets become practical applications of the laws in scripture.

By learning the laws in scripture, and the lessons taught by the prophets, a disciple of Scripture emulates what it means to be Christ-like. We cannot know the person who was Christ, but we have the Holy Bible that records the life and experiences of the person who is Christ. We have the red words, which are those spoken by Jesus Christ when He was here.

To the disciple of Scripture, the red words are the most Christ-like expressions left on earth. The art and science of weaving those red words into the laws and lessons of the prophets bring a spiritual presence to the world that has not been seen since the apostles took on the Great Commission.

A disciple of Scripture loves to help people. Through many years of study, decades of life's experiences, and helping people, the Holy Spirit of God flows through the disciple of Scripture and accomplishes God's purpose in the world.

Being a disciple of Scripture is more than just reading the Bible. It is understanding what the message means and how to apply it in everyday life. It is having an active vocabulary of scripture that is very large. The ability to reconcile what is going on in the world today, in people's lives every day, with the laws and lessons of the prophets in scripture.

When a disciple of Scripture offers advice, it is not a personal judgment but a compass for behavior written down for us in scripture. There is no divine appointment necessary to become a disciple of Scripture. It is a personal choice. It takes a sustained effort over time. It is not a job per se. It is a part of one's personal devotion to God and scripture.

A person's faith in God will manifest itself in that person's life. If we know the scriptures, we know what God is capable of. He is all-knowing, all-powerful, everywhere at once in all times. There are no secrets before Him; no lie can stand in His presence. If He is on your side, the enemy is doomed.

By the same token, a person's lack of faith will also manifest itself in their life. If they do not know scripture, they do not know what God is capable of. They think they are able to keep secrets, that no one can discern their lies, and that there will be no accountability at the end of physical life.

The disciple of Scripture knows both sides of human nature. While comfortable in their own relationship with their Creator, they know it is a calling of faith to witness and spread the word when possible.

# Chapter 4

## FAITH VS. RELIGION

I am going to define religion and faith.

Webster's New World College Dictionary, fourth edition, defines religion: reverence for the gods, holiness. 1) A system of religious belief, belief in a divine or superhuman power or powers to be obeyed and worshiped as the creator(s) and ruler(s) of the universe. 1) Expression of such belief in conduct and ritual.

Notice the word *faith* does not appear in the definition of religion.

Faith: 1) unquestioning belief that does not require proof or evidence. 2) Unquestioning belief in God, religious tenets, etc. 3) A religion or system of religious beliefs. 4) Anything believed. 5) Complete trust, confidence, or reliance.

Bearing those definitions in mind, when I was much younger, I was a person of religion. In my religion, it was expected of me, "by *me*," to follow certain religious views. I listened to the priests during Sunday mass and took to heart their message. I didn't read the Bible for myself to know the scriptures. My expectations in religion conditionally changed my behavior.

Much as a person in religion doesn't want to sin. The challenge is such people do not know the scriptures for themselves. They take the word of the preacher that they are okay spiritually.

One of my experiences as a grade schooler was this. I became curious about scripture. I asked questions like, "When God said let us create man in our own image, who was He speaking to?" Another question I had was, "If Adam and Eve had only two sons, and one killed the other, where did the killer find a wife?" Also, "What was the mark God put on the killer so no one else would afflict him?" "Why would he fear that if only his mom and dad were left?"

The nuns that taught the class couldn't answer me. The kids in class fed off what they perceived as my rebellion, and class became unruly. I was sent to the principal's office. The father came in, and I repeated my questions for him. He answered me in Latin. I do not understand Latin, so that irritated me even more. After the school informed my parents about my disruptive behavior in class and my brazen disrespect for all authority, my parents elected to take me out of that school.

What this example illustrates is religious leaders are more concerned about the doctrine of their religion than the text of scripture. My answers to the questions are: God was speaking to the host of heaven, Cain found a wife many years after the murder, I still don't know what the mark is, and he feared reprisals because the first murder was probably very traumatic.

What I share with you in this work is scripture-based faith, not religion.

To deal with the extra hassle of self-imposed expectations, people convince themselves it is something that they want personally. They make themselves "tolerate" the change to achieve the goal. Then they will revert to their normal pattern of behavior when changing conditions relieve those self-imposed expectations.

Faith is different. You can own a Bible and take it anywhere. You can read when you want. You can read as much or as little as you want. It can sit there for days undisturbed. You can read from it every day. Everything that you read will build your scriptural database. For me, I learned a lot of things I didn't know in the first year of reading the Bible for myself.

Many years ago, my stepson was very much against going to church on Sundays. I asked him to explain where this feeling came from. He told me the services he had experienced made him feel bad about himself. He was told he was bad because all men were sinners. Then the church tried to guilt trip him into giving his money to the church. Then the priest would talk about something he didn't really see any value in knowing. Then the priest told everybody to get out of his church.

I summed up his feelings like this: "Church to you is, you're a sinner, you're bad, give us your money, now get out?"

My stepson looked at me with an expression of "eureka!" His stepdad finally understood how church made him feel. I wasn't prepared to deal with that in the moment. I told him then that I understood how he felt and that he could skip church until I figured out something different. I urged him to read the Bible for himself so he knew what it said.

The story made its rounds through the whole family. The consensus was my stepson was right about how church services were conducted. How does a parent convince their child that a personal relationship with *God* is very beneficial to them? Religious doctrine and dogma stifle the free flow of the Holy Spirit from God to the believer. I heard a saying that resonated with me. It concerns this issue of faith versus religion. In my mind, I see the person of faith speaking to religious institutions, "Your dogma got ran over by my karma."

When I see the difference in the way I feel between being told what the Bible says and reading it for myself, I do not want to go back to the way it was.

My mother once told me she tried to read the Bible for herself, but it just made her more confused. Her question to me was, "Where do I start reading the Bible so it makes sense?" I used to read a chapter from the Old and New Testaments every day. Once I finished either section, I started it over. In that way, I read the Bible several times. Now I just read from cover to cover and start over.

I "expected" my mother, the one who introduced me to religion when I was a child, to know that was what people of faith did. After getting my head around the concept that my own mother was not a regular Bible reader, my interest in the self-imposed expectation phenomenon grew.

What do you say to a person you love and respect, who has a serious need to know, and you just want to say, "Do what I do"? I think differently than either my stepson or my mother. I am more of a legalistic person. I want to know the rules. When I know the rules, I am not afraid to challenge the authorities when I believe they are the ones violating the rules.

When I don't know the rules, I cannot state my own case effectively. It is the same for everyone. I have seen that self-imposed expectation phenomenon work against people. People who really want to have faith but get little or no help. The self-imposed expectation kicks in, and the person affected goes without experiencing the rewards of scripture-based faith. I don't like to see that.

What I am looking for is a way to be positive, encouraging, and uplifting so more people can experience the joy of confidence in knowing they are walking a scripturally accurate path before almighty God.

As often happens in the exploration of faith, almost by accident, something new comes to light. It is filled with its own light and shines more brightly on the path you walk. It was unknown, at least by me at the time. I didn't know I was missing it. Only when it became obvious did I see it clearly.

How do we prevent ourselves from putting expectations on ourselves? We must have a serious heart-to-heart talk with ourselves. There is what we need and what we want. Some things we can control, other things we can influence, and the rest are just things we are concerned about. We need to focus on our needs and what we can control first.

We don't have the power to change our hearts. Only *God* can do that.

How do we change when we think we are already doing the best we can? If we are experiencing a range of success, we think working harder will make things better. That is a death trap.

My father once told me, "There is such a thing as dead right."

At the time, I was a teenager. That time in my life when I had all the answers. My father saw I was not being reasonable. Instead of engaging in a hurtful exchange of words, he showed me a possibility I hadn't considered. I wondered out loud, "If you are right, how can you die?"

My dad answered, "A lot of people had the green light and died in traffic accidents. They are asking *God* the same question."

That "dead right" example applies to the scripture, "Do not be unequally yoked with unbelievers" (2 Corinthians 6:14, BSB). I had read it before, many times. I used it in teaching my children and grandchildren about people without the same morals and values, trying to take advantage of people who play by the rules.

With this seemingly impossible conundrum of self-imposed expectations still working its way around my mind, the scripture took on a new meaning. *God* knows the world is home to nonbelievers. He gave us that scripture for dealing with them. Not in a physical act way, but as a matter of faith.

Now I am contemplating life as a person trying to grow my personal relationship with *God*. I still want to turn the table on the world and the worldly people in it. Faith in Jesus Christ is that turning of the tables. The evil one gets what he has been prophesized to get (Revelation 20:10). We get the blessings *God* intended for us (Genesis 49:25). Jesus said, "Greater love has no one than this, that he lay down his life for his friends" (John 15:13, BSB). He died for us on the cross. Jesus prayed for us (John 17:20, NLT). Jesus went to prepare a place for us and promised to return for us (John 14:3).

The devil is real. The Bible tells us he tempted Jesus in the wilderness. The devil afflicted Job. We are told the devil accuses all before *God* (Zechariah 3:1–2, Job 1:6–7, Revelation 12:10). Somebody new to biblical faith is quickly overwhelmed with all the history, places, people, and events in the Bible. The devil knows this and uses it to his advantage.

How bad could it be? It is horribly bad (2 Corinthians 2:10–11)! The first thing that I think is important to know is that *God* intended for *His* creation to remain in paradise with *Him* for eternity. My justification for that is found in scripture. *God* made us in *His* image (Genesis 1:27). *He* put Adam and Eve in paradise (Genesis 2:8). When they sinned, *God* had to punish them (Genesis 3:3–19). Then *God* sent His only-begotten Son as a ransom for all who will believe in Him (John 3:16). *God* didn't have to do this. It provides a way for us to get back to the paradise we lost.

Even though it is possible to be reconciled back to *God* through Jesus Christ, we have work to do. We are subject to curses. Not only the ones that resulted from the fall of Adam and Eve. We have a limited life expectancy of one hundred and twenty years (Genesis 6:3).

That is not the first curse *God* placed upon humankind. When Adam and Eve sinned in the Garden of Eden by eating the forbidden fruit, they provoked several curses. They were kicked out of paradise.

They were excommunicated from *God's* presence. The man was to till the earth by the sweat of his brow, but it would yield little to him. He was going to have to deal with thorn and thistle. All these and more were completely alien concepts to both Adam and Eve the day they ate the forbidden fruit (Genesis 3:14–19).

Eve was cursed, the serpent was cursed, and the earth was cursed. There are more. After Moses led the Israelites out of bondage in Egypt as a holy man of *God*, more curses followed. In the wilderness, while Moses was on Mount Sinai receiving the first copy of the Ten Commandments, the Israelites made themselves a golden calf and worshipped it.

As a result, a long litany of curses was declared by *God* against *His* human creation. Deuteronomy chapter 28, verses 1 to 14, are the blessing for obedience to *God*. Verses 15 to 68 are the curses for disobedience to *God*. (A lot more curses than blessings.) The condition that brings the curses upon us is disobedience to *God*. We live under them whether we know it or not. Belief in them is irrelevant. Ignorance of the law has no effect.

If we do not learn from the hardship of these curses, if we persist in our disobedience to *God*, then *God* will "gave them [us] over to a reprobate mind" (Romans 1:28–32, KJV). (Hereinafter, brackets added for clarity.) When that happens, the sinner is bound for punishment in eternity.

If we make an effort and make mistakes, we must keep trying. Keep smiling and keep trying. I have never heard this type of message from any church I attended. If I had, it would be the church of choice for me.

The only way I learned these things was by reading the scriptures for myself. My scripture-based faith led me to these secrets of success in my faith. I want everyone who is willing to put their own time and effort into reading scripture to do so and see what develops. It takes a sustained effort over time, but this guide will help readers get the most out of it as quickly as possible.

# Chapter 5

## BELIEF OR BEREFT

How do people think about God? Let me qualify this statement in this way:

Many people pray to God to win the lottery so they can finally be happy in this life.

Such people put too much emphasis on the money being able to make them happy and not enough emphasis on the happiness God can bring them. It is asking God to give you happiness but excluding God from the happy picture. That is why prayers to win the lottery do not work.

I wonder if other people are like me. When the jackpot gets to a certain point, over $500 million, I buy a ticket for the next drawing. All the while I am waiting for that drawing, I am preoccupied with what I will do with the money *if* I am the only winner of the over $500 million prize! During this time, I don't even consider any lesser prize. So many thoughts come to my mind about how I would spend *all that money*! It is literally already spent before the drawing even happens. Then I don't win, and I feel like I have a hangover for a while.

"Does that happen to anyone else?" "So, I am more normal than I want to admit?" I have heard that before!

What we think, how we think it, and how much time and effort we put into our thinking are open to God for His inspection all the time. If we are not thinking about God, goodness, and how to be a blessing to others, He knows it. It doesn't matter what we say out loud to make ourselves sound better. He knows our private, innermost thoughts. He knows our secret motives and hidden intentions. The plans we form behind the words we use are an open book for God to read.

I used to wonder how that was possible. Then I realized the spirit that is dwelling within us is from God. It is experiencing what we experience. It sees what we see, hears what we hear, and knows what we know. It also knows God is its true master and wants to be obedient to God. It is a spirit trapped in human flesh. If the person is obedient, I believe the spirit from God is happy within that human body. I also believe if the person is disobedient to God, the spirit from God dwelling in that flesh is very unhappy.

How else can God know our minds and hearts? His spirit is in us, recording it all live in real time. That is why I believe people when they say they had out-of-body experience (OBE) or near-death experience (NDE). The spirit within them was outside their body for a moment. It recorded the memory it saw. Then it returned to the body, and the body now remembers that memory also.

Another persuasive story is Edgar Cayce's story. As a child, he read the Bible a dozen times and prayed for and was visited by an angel whom he told he wanted to help people. (Any of this sounding familiar?) As a result, Edgar Cayce became known as *the sleeping prophet*. He would pray and meditate until he was in a semiconscious state, and then someone close to him would ask him questions. He would answer from his meditative state, and the answers he gave were remarkably accurate. He revealed that he got his answers from the Akashic records. These are what I believe scripture calls the *heavenly books of knowledge*. The recordings of what every human spirit has recorded in its service to God. The following twenty scriptures refer to written records that will witness to God about human conduct: Exodus 32:32–33; Psalm 56:8, 69:28, 139:16; Ezekiel 13:9; Daniel

7:10, 12:1; Isaiah 65:6; Malachi 3:16; Luke 10:20; Philippians 4:3; Hebrews 12:23; Revelation 3:5, 5:1, 13:8, 17:8, 20:12, 15, 21:27, 22:18–19.

Daniel 7:10, Revelation 17:8, and Revelation 20:12 are especially poignant. From these scriptures, we know those writings do exist, they are in heaven, and God will refer to them. Each person will have to give account for themselves, their thoughts, words, and deeds from all their life. If they are not confessing with their mouth, if they have not written a confession, how does God obtain the record? We know it is there. We know there is a spirit in each person that is from God and goes back to God when the physical body expires. It makes sense that spirit is the writer of the personal record.

For a disciple of Scripture, this is blatantly obvious. It ties together all the mysteries of divine omnipotence when it comes to human interaction and judgment for it. How else can a perfect judgment be reached? We have all the evidence recorded live from the point of view of the accused, and it is publicly displayed in the court of heaven. The secret thoughts of the accused are displayed as subtitles in a movie. The desires of the heart are shown in a sidebar running along with the actual events. Even the accused will be convinced of their sin(s).

That is the eventuality the disciple of Scripture wants to be prepared for. Out of the love in their heart for helping others, they want to share this knowledge with anyone who will listen. Every person has to go through this process. We will all stand in judgment. We will be judged and have to give account. How each one of us will do is between self and Creator. Being honest with yourself is now the best policy for entering the grace of God. No false pretense will prevail when the secret thoughts and desires of the heart are shown along with the actual events in real time. "It is written..."

# Chapter 6

## GROWING FAITH

The first particle of faith is believing in God. This tiny amount of faith is enough for God to work with. It is not a competition; it is not a race. It doesn't matter how much or how little faith is perceived by others, for others, or in others. Faith is a private relationship between the believer and their Creator.

We do not have to understand any amount of scripture to have this faith.

We do not have to abide by every single law in scripture to have this faith.

We do not have to know all the lessons taught by the prophets in the Bible to have this faith.

If a person can say, "God, I know You are there..." that is enough faith.

"And it is impossible to please God without faith. Anyone who wants to come to him must believe that God exists and that he rewards those who sincerely seek him" (Hebrews 11:6, NLT).

If a new believer exercises the smallest particle of faith by praying to God, reading the Bible, going to church, acting with charity to help someone without the expectation of payment, or asking a person of faith questions about their faith, these things are exercising faith. It leads to a greater knowledge of what faith means.

The one who taught me asked me, "Do you know how I knew you were ready to hear the Word of God?"

I remember being very angry at God at that time; I answered no. He said, "Because you kept asking me questions about scripture."

That was enough for God to nurture the faith I had when I was still very angry at God.

"But solid food is for the mature, who by constant use have trained their senses to distinguish good from evil" (Hebrews 5:14, NIV).

How did my faith in God manifest when I was arguing with God? The fact that I believed He caused my pain was an admission of His existence. I believed in Him, even though I was blaming Him for my troubles. If God can take that small bit of faith and, over twenty-eight years, grow it into the faith I have now, He can do the same and even more for anyone.

"And now, just as you accepted Christ Jesus as your Lord, you must continue to follow him. Let your roots grow down into him, and let your lives be built on him. Then your faith will grow strong in the truth you were taught, and you will overflow with thankfulness" (Colossians 2:6–7, NLT).

There is always hope. There is no person too dirty for God to cleanse. There is no person too broken for God to fix. There is no circumstance too difficult for God. The trick for us is to put God first in our lives. I can tell you from personal experience I thought burning the Bible was an unforgivable sin. I thought telling God I didn't believe in Him was unforgivable. I thought blaming God for my suffering was unforgivable. If none of those were truly unforgivable, then I knew for sure claiming to be God myself was unforgivable. Just to be clear, I admitted to it, I asked God to forgive me for it, and He has.

*So let us stop going over the basic teachings about Christ again and again. Let us go on instead and become mature in our understanding. Surely we don't need to start again with the fundamental importance of repenting from evil deeds and placing our faith in God. You don't need further instruction about baptisms, the laying on of hands, the resurrection of the dead, and eternal judgment. And so, God willing, we will move forward to further understanding.*

Hebrews 6:1–3 (NLT)

The statement, "I am going to do things my way, and I don't care what the consequences are," cost me a great deal of shame, pain, and guilt. The important thing to take away from my testimony is, I did a lot of terrible things, all of which have been forgiven.

How do I know? After I paroled from prison, my mom and stepdad took me in. I was given a fresh start. I had to get a job and pay my share of the expenses. I did that. From that humble beginning as a free person, God's blessings rained down on me like the monsoon.

I still was not perfect. I still fell to sin many times. But I asked God to forgive me every time and keep blessing me. Eventually, I was married to a wonderful woman of God. I had a family, a nice vehicle, a decent home, a six-figure income, and I was not worried about getting stopped by law enforcement for any reason. The worst thing I could get in trouble for was speeding. No warrants, I owned the vehicle, my name was on the registration, I had proof of insurance, and my license was current and active.

"Because of the privilege and authority God has given me, I give each of you this warning: Don't think you are better than you really are. Be honest in your evaluation of yourselves, measuring yourselves by the faith God has given us" (Romans 12:3, NLT).

There is the requirement that we must exercise our faith.

When I look back to that day in the prison cell in 1994, I never would have hoped to have it so good, ever, after my parole. I have been able to pass on my faith to my stepchildren and grandchildren. Seeing them grow and blossom is a blessing.

Has my life been trouble-free since 1994? No, it has not. I am just better prepared for life's bumps and wrong turns. I have learned it is much more about how I react to a situation than the situation itself. One example I give is this:

You get a flat tire while driving on vacation. You get the flat one off the car, put the donut on, and as you go to collect the lug nuts, you tip the hub cap, and all the lug nuts fall and roll into the sewer. What do you do now?

Well, you still have three other tires with all their lug nuts, right? Take one lug nut off each of the other three tires and secure the donut tire with them. It will be a good enough fix until you can replace the tire and lug nuts.

The reaction to the situation is key. If you had a serious rage fit over losing the lug nuts down the sewer, how would that help your situation? It would not. You might give yourself a stroke or aneurism. It is not worth it.

Many things in life are this way. In the moment the event is happening, we may not see the solution clearly. The process is to accept it, understand what it really is, and begin searching for the solution.

*For I know the plans I have for you, declares the LORD, plans to prosper you and not to harm you, to give you a future and a hope. Then you will call upon Me and come and pray to Me, and I will listen to you. You will seek Me and find Me when you search for Me with all your heart.*

Jeremiah 29:11–13 (BSB)

I was once asked a question on an oral and practical exam. We were supposed to give the most accurate answer. The question I got was, "There is an oil leak coming from one engine of your twin-engine aircraft; what do you do about it?"

I began my answer with: "It depends on the situation. If we are in a combat zone and about to be overrun by the enemy, I will fly it to allied territory or as close as it can make it. If we are in Wichita Falls flying a commuter airline for hire, we must fix the leak before we go anywhere."

The proctor was open-minded enough to recognize my answer was good for the perceived situation. When he clarified the situation, it was a private aircraft, and the oil had recently been changed, that changed my answer.

The point is every person alive looks at things through their own eyes. They notice things in a unique way. When we exercise our faith, it is the same way. Our walk of faith is distinguishable from that of other people. It does not make us better or worse; it makes us unique. If we were all the exact same, life would be so boring.

*Now may the God of hope fill you with all joy and peace as you believe in Him, so that you may overflow with hope by the power of the Holy Spirit. I myself am convinced, my brothers, that you yourselves are full of goodness, brimming with knowledge, and able to instruct one another.*

Romans 15:13–14 (BSB)

It is the great diversity of people in faith that give us our strength. Our brothers and sisters in faith can approach us in our common faith and say, "I prayed for you, and the Lord gave me a word for you." This is how we approach instructing one another in faith.

"All Scripture is God-breathed and is useful for instruction, for conviction, for correction, and for training in righteousness, so that the man of God may be complete, fully equipped for every good work" (2 Timothy 3:16–17, BSB).

# Chapter 7

## PUNISHMENT AND REWARD

If our punishment for disobedience is eternal, will our reward for obedience also last forever? What I am about to tell you is the key to enjoying a better life through faith in *God*. The secret knowledge is this, "We are playing for eternity!"

Let that sink in for a moment. We are, by faith, living our life so that we regain the paradise lost when Adam and Eve were disobedient to God in the Garden of Eden. That paradise for human existence is what *God* intended for us. That was our "first estate." Adam and Eve, breaking *God's* only rule, forced *God* to punish them and, by proxy, us.

Adam knew the price for disobedience; *God* told him, "you will surely die" (Genesis 2:17, BSB).

Before that "*original sin*," we were in paradise; we did live for eternity; we were with *God*. There was no sickness, pain, hunger, or shame. There was no guilt for anything. That is what *God* intended for *His* creation.

Adam and Eve were disobedient. There are many more examples throughout the Old Testament explaining how humankind failed to live up to *God's* expectations for us. We have the *God*-given tools to know right from wrong. *God's* laws are written on the tablets of our hearts (2 Corinthians 3:3). We already know what we need to do. It is only a matter of embracing that knowledge. We can order our thoughts to choose our words and actions out of free will. Our choice in what we say or do is the exercise of free will (Deuteronomy

11:26–28, NLT). We will be held accountable for every word we speak (Matthew 12:36) and every deed we do (Ecclesiastes 12:14).

Because the devil is such a potent enemy, no matter what we do, the devil wants us to fail. The devil will use every tool in his *infernal arsenal* to bring us down. Things like doubt and fear. The devil knows if we doubt *God* is in charge, we are susceptible to temptation and sin. The devil knows if we fear anything else more than we fear provoking *God's* wrath on us, we are an easy target.

The devil has the seven deadly sins to tempt us with. The devil knows the seven things that *God* hates. The devil knows the fruits of the vineyard of the wicked. He knows us. He plants those stray thoughts in our minds. It is up to us to recognize them for what they are and call them out. We are told to "test the spirits" (1 John 4:1–4). Those stray thoughts that just pop in our heads from time to time are not sin. They are the tricks of the devil seeking to catch us in a snare. If we act on those stray thoughts, that becomes our sin. The devil delights in causing us to fall in that way.

I have been in prayer, meditating on a particular scripture to *God*, and strange thoughts interrupt my prayer and meditation. It happens when I am reading the Bible. It happens when I am praying out loud. It is the evidence of evil spirits attacking me and my faith. To combat them, I rebuke the enemy in the name of Jesus Christ, my Lord and Savior. It causes those thoughts to stop. The devil is nothing if not persistent. The attacks begin anew whenever my focus drifts away from the absolute supremacy of *God*. That is why we are told to pray continuously (1 Thessalonians 5:17).

The devil has even more subtle tricks for us. Many times, in our walk of faith, we start out on a course of action with good intentions. As we progress in those efforts, the set of circumstances we started with begins to change. I am reminded of a scene from the movie *Star Wars: The Empire Strikes Back*. The scene is the one where Lando Calrissian is talking to Darth Vader about the deal they struck just before Han Solo arrived at Cloud City. The quote is by Vader to Lando, "Pray I don't alter the deal any further." Vader was the devil's advocate there.

The devil knows that once we get into a project, we don't want to let anything prevent its completion. We deal with the worsening conditions as best we can. Some projects get to be such a hassle that we either scrub the whole plan or drastically alter the original goal. That is the devil altering the deal little by little every chance he gets.

The devil is not alone in his efforts to cause humans to sin. In the battle for heaven, Lucifer drew one-third of the host of heaven to his side (Revelation 12:4). The host of heaven is an infinite number. More than the grains of sand under the sea and in all the deserts around world. They fought a war against God, and the rest of the host of heaven over the new creation, humankind.

To say they are bitter about being defeated, cursed to eternal suffering, and cast down to earth is a gross understatement. They know they cannot defeat God. They already suffered for trying that. Now they pick on the creation. From the tower of Babel to the Flood of Noah, to Sodom and Gomorrah, and many more, the fallen angels have afflicted humankind with every vice, hate, and fruit of the vineyard of the wicked. They know the scripture as well as anyone. They have seen humankind from the Garden of Eden until today. They have perfected their strategies and tactics against humankind throughout human history. They celebrate every sin they cause. Scripture says the devil comes to steal, kill, and destroy (John 10:10).

That is what the devil wants to accomplish. He wants us to get discouraged and quit fighting him. Our motivation to keep fighting is we can be forgiven for our mistakes; we do not have to be perfect (1 John 1:9).

No matter how bad we are cheated, we need to keep our faith and trust in *God*. We are to pray for those who hurt us (Matthew 5:43–44, Romans 12:14). It helps me, and I hope you can come to the same conclusion, we can work around the devil's attempts to stifle our faith and the stumbling blocks he sets in our path. Faith in Jesus Christ, a more accurate understanding of scripture, and playing for eternity are the answers.

Most people in the modern world have learned that financial success is the gateway to every good thing we can possibly imagine. That is true only in a worldly sense. As stated above, in faith, we are playing for eternity, not just wealth and the stuff and things money can buy here on earth. We want to also store up our treasures in heaven.

"No eye has seen, no ear has heard, no heart has imagined, what GOD has prepared for those who love *Him*" (1 Corinthians 2:9, NLT). (Hereinafter, emphasis added.) I want to point out that Jesus Christ came from Heaven to earth. He was in the battle for heaven and defeated Lucifer and his rebellious angels. He knew what *God's* creation was missing by giving into sin. He wanted to show us by example that eternity in paradise with *God* was worth everything he suffered.

He lived a normal human life for thirty years before He began His ministry. He came from a working-class family of modest means. Life happened for Him and His family all those first thirty years. He lived with Roman occupation under the rule of King Herod and with the corrupt politics of the Sanhedrin. He experienced human existence as most people on earth did at the time.

All his life, He never sinned. His trouble came from the corrupt politics of the religious leaders of the time (Matthew 5:20). They could not accept a savior that did not destroy all the enemies of the religion. Jesus Christ was betrayed by a member of His inner circle. He was abducted from the Garden of Gethsemane in the middle of the night. He was put through a mock trial in a private home of one of those who hated Him at night! (Not in a courtroom with a defense attorney and an official charge under law.) They convicted Him of being the Son of *God*! I wonder what they had to say after *His* resurrection.

The religious leaders who plotted to kill Jesus when he walked this earth lived in luxury. They set the value of their rank or station as well as their stuff and things above the value of other people. Jesus preached that people were more important. If the religious leaders didn't understand that, they would not inherit eternal life. They traded their comforts in life for a place in paradise (Luke 6:24). My understanding of it is that people who value their wealth, stuff, and things more than they value other people and/or their faith will not inherit paradise. Hence the scripture, "It is easier for a camel to pass through the eye of a needle than it is for a rich man to enter the kingdom of God" (Mark 10:25, BSB).

Some people of wealth would probably be glad to trade their wealth for eternity in paradise, but that is not how it works with *God*. No one can purchase *God's* blessings. The attempt to do so is called Simmonism. Simon the Sorcerer was denied access to the growing church ministry for attempting to buy *God's* blessings from the Apostle Peter in the book of Acts chapter 8, verses 18 to 20.

What that tells us is wealth is nothing in the eyes of *God*. It is the people who matter. People are *God's* creation. What humans make or the possessions they accumulate do nothing unless they praise and glorify *God*. Those works will count for us. The rest is all detrimental.

Some people like to think that punishment should fit the crime. That is a human legalistic perception. According to scripture, either an offender can make restitution, or they cannot. In scripture, restitution can be made for property crimes but not for murder (Numbers 35:30–31).

The spoken word has power. When we speak scriptures in pursuit of our faith, *God* hears. The devil and his minions hear it also (James 2:19). The word of *God* does not return void (Isaiah 55:11). The scriptures are the words of *God*. They are what Jesus Christ spoke when tempted in the wilderness. Every answer Jesus gave the devil contained the phrase, "It is written..." (Matthew 4:4)

That is our example of how to answer the devil when we are tempted. If you don't know a single Bible verse, try saying, "Lord have mercy!" *He* knows what we are going through. *He* sees into our hearts and minds. *He* knows we are at a severe disadvantage when we first start our walk in faith. Part of our faith test is whether we believe strongly enough to put *God* first in our lives.

In 2008, my wife and I made a pact with each other. We mutually decided in faith that we both needed to put *God* first in our lives. Both of us are strong in our faith, and we realize that each of us needs to be right with *God* before we can be right with anyone else. That made us see ourselves being second in our personal chain of faith. Then we both said our vows to each other in the house of *God* before an ordained minister and the whole congregation. That meant spouse was third in our personal chain of faith. *God*, self, and spouse—that is the order.

Being a believer married to a believer is such a blessing. Our marriage blossomed from our commitment to support each other in faith and put *God* first. We spoke of scripture when dealing with every decision. What does scripture say about what we are experiencing? We would pray together and ask *God* to lead, guide, and direct us. We found ourselves amid calm tranquility. We worked hard at our jobs and became financially secure for the first time in our lives. Not because we made so much money, but because we found contentedness in the things we could afford. If our finances could barely cover the monthly bills, we were happy to be able to go another month with all that we had.

When our jobs demanded overtime to be worked, we budgeted as if the overtime money was not there. Just the regular forty-hour-a-week income is what we used for a budget. When the overtime went away, we had a financial cushion in the bank. That peace of mind made unexpected bills less traumatic monetarily.

We committed to giving our tithes every payday. Our financial troubles dissipated. We used to tell each other, "We don't have any problems a little more money couldn't fix." We were soon telling struggling family members, "The *Lord* has blessed us; we can be a blessing to you."

We went into a stage of life that can only be described as living right. We both worked, and our children were adults getting married and starting families of their own. Our home and cars were paid off. We had accumulated plenty of vacation time. For the first time, we experienced the ability to plan our next vacation as soon as we came home from the most recent one. That means we took our vacation and came back with vacation still on the books, time to plan another vacation!

Our romance quotient was very high. Many of our friends saw us and said we gave them a toothache from how sweet we were to each other. They compared us to a couple who recently met and were still in the infatuation stage of their relationship. We had been married for many years at the time.

People in the family would ask us for advice. We would go to the Bible. We began to see a pattern develop. Those people who took the scriptural guidance to heart seemed to do well. Those who tried something else didn't do so well. We prayed for all of them. We even prayed a special prayer of a ten percent increase back to those who were praying for us.

Our lives were good. We still had the stuff of everyday life. Life happens, but it didn't get to us like it did before we committed ourselves to God first. Through the years, I lost a brother to addiction, a stepbrother to disease, a grandchild to a drunk driver, and my stepfather to the legacy of *Agent Orange*. There was unjustly inflicted pain and suffering even during the "good times."

We were asked how we deal with the tragedies in our lives and keep our faith alive. Our lives were about to change, and that change was going to demonstrate our faith and endurance. While doing my research for this book, my wife found a lump in her right breast. We prayed a lot, got on every prayer chain we found, and sought the best medical treatment possible. She did a great deal of research on her treatment options. When she found something especially edifying, she shared it with me.

The process took nearly ten years. From a biopsy to a lumpectomy to years of vigilant breast exams to a mastectomy and a radical mastectomy before the cancer metastasized. We supported each other in faith and everyday life. It was a terrifying time in our life. We clung to God in our faith no matter what life threw at us.

Before cancer, we both worked at good-paying jobs in our chosen career fields. These jobs also had good benefits. We had an incredible family life and many good friendships. We were active in our church. We traveled on vacation twice a year. We had an amazing love life. Both of us looked forward to our golden years together.

During the battle with cancer, the hardest thing for me was seeing the disease rob my wife of her sexy. A woman's breasts are a strong personal identity factor. Having two breasts is very important to her self-image and self-esteem. She compared it to a man losing his testicles, but that is not as easy to discern as a woman missing a breast.

Making a play on the term "one-hit wonder," I very affectionately told her, "You are my one-breast wonder. I love you more with one breast than any other woman with two breasts."

She smiled and thanked me for the sentiment, but it did little to cheer her up.

Every step of the way, we pulled together. God was first in both of our lives. After God, we worked on ourselves and our understanding of scripture and our personal relationship with God. The third priority for both of us was our spouse.

We prayed for her complete healing. For her to go into remission. For the Rapture to happen so we could go together. For her to be at peace and experience no suffering.

We did say all the things to each other that we needed to. I was there with her through her dying breath. When she passed, she was surrounded by her family in her home. Her favorite inspirational songs were playing. Our pastor was praying over her. I did everything for her as she wanted it.

When you are there with a loved one in faith, and you feel their spirit rise out of their body, it is bittersweet. You know they are going to paradise, and you must wait your turn without them. For a long time, I felt like I was robbed of thirty years with my soulmate. I did not understand why God allowed this to happen, but I knew He was the author of our lives. Like it or not, understand it or not, God knows better than we do.

One of our pastors told me, "We don't know what God was saving her from." It makes sense when you realize that everyone will pass. Not everyone truly gets to enjoy their life. We did. Whatever God's plan is, I feel blessed for the experiences I have.

There was a point during this years-long battle when I prayed for God to show me what life in heaven would be like. After praying that prayer, I had a very vivid dream.

In this dream, I found myself walking in a landscape of rolling hills. At the top of each hill was a fountain of fresh water. The water flowed downhill to irrigate small gardens. Each garden was equal in size. There was a small orchard in each. The water flowed between the rows of trees in each garden. Then the water flowed around many kinds of food plants in their rows. There was a patch of green grass in each garden that looked good for a place to rest. As I looked around in this dream, I saw a brilliant golden light shining upon all things. As my eyes adjusted to the light, I could see rows of hills receding into the great distance beyond the horizon in every direction.

While seeing this vision, I felt a sense of great awe. There was a surreal feeling of warmth, energy resonating from everything to everything, unconditional love, and security in this place. When I looked to the crest of the far hills and wondered what the view would be from there, I felt as if I was flying. Almost instantly, I landed safely in the spot I was looking at and wondering about. The hills seemed to have no end.

I realized each small garden was like the Garden of Eden. It was a perfect habitation for people. There was a steady supply of fresh water and food. The people that were there each occupied a single garden. They were free to move around and mingle. Their eyes glowed with energy. Their bodies glowed as if filled with an inner light. Every person's countenance exuded joy and happiness. In the moment, I felt this place was home. Then the vision faded, and I woke from my dream.

My wife was still alive when I had this dream. I told her about it. She got goosebumps on her arms, and she shivered when I did. All she said was, "Sounds like paradise." She did enjoy her gardens as long as she was healthy enough to do so.

In the immediate aftermath of her passing, I felt lost. Everything we did was aimed at saving her life. Then it became prolonging her life. After that, it was about giving her the best quality of life for the time she had left. Then it was all about making her comfortable until the end.

My answer to the question of how I go through a tragedy and keep my faith alive is, "My courage to continue living life is greater than my fear of being hurt again." How did I come by this courage? The courage I have came from my realization that too many things did not make sense during the tragedy of cancer. When you believe that God loves us and will take care of us, how is it taking care of us to have things like cancer in our world? We prayed very diligently, the most powerful prayers we knew how to pray. We were on every prayer chain we could find. We changed many things in our everyday habits to be as healthy as possible. This was almost a decade-long battle. We changed what we did to adapt to the circumstances as best we understood them.

That very undesirable negative outcome kept creeping closer. We refused to give up. We had to set our sights on a different hope. We are both saved. Our greatest hope is to receive God's grace and attain eternal life in paradise with God. The only way we can do that, go to heaven, is to give up our earthly existence.

As difficult as that is, we believe physical existence is temporary anyway. We also believe that the spiritual existence is eternal. We would consider it a good trade if we got a new replacement for anything else we had if that thing was old and about to fail. Our spiritual body will last for eternity; is that not a better deal for us?

Letting go of our attachment to the physical existence is a source of fear, doubt, distraction, and selfish pursuits. Those are the weapons of the enemy. To see past our fears, doubts, distractions, and selfish pursuits, we must cling to the faith that our spiritual existence will be better. If we believe we are saved, that is a lot easier.

It stands to reason that the enemy of God would want to shroud the afterlife in fear and doubt. We are the closest to heaven we can get when we are exiting our physical existence. The enemy doesn't want us to go that way. He wants us to blame God for our misery and sin against God. We cannot do that. We must fear God's wrath worse than death. We must never doubt that God is all-powerful and can do anything. We must never be so distracted that serving God first is impossible for us. We cannot be so selfish that our temporary physical form means more to us than our eternal spiritual form.

When my wife accepted her terminal condition, she said, "I am ready to meet Jesus. I want to see again those who have gone before us."

That caused our focus to shift from God allowing the disease to destroy her physical form to the eternal reward for a good and faithful servant. Faithful even to death. God was not allowing her to suffer this horrible disease; He was calling her home. She was a very good person. Everyone who knew her loved her. She would help anybody in any way she could. She was smart, funny, and could work circles around almost anyone. Why would God take her out of the world so soon? Because He judged that she had earned her angel's wings. It hurt me. I will carry the scar for the rest of my life. I know I must be good *and* obtain the grace of God if I am going to meet her in heaven.

When you love someone that much, it is hard to think of them being better off without you. Jesus Christ died for her. He came back from the dead to make sure she could go to heaven. It is the same for all of us. Jesus wants to save everyone. We must claim Him for that to work. Once we claim Him, we can never let go. He will not let us go. No other force in the universe can take us from Him. The only way we can separate from Him is by turning away from Him. If we keep trying to do good and keep faith in Jesus Christ, we can never be too dirty, too broken, or too far away for Jesus to save us.

The result of my belief is I carry a lot of scars with me. Life-changing events never get any better. Only great amounts of time distance us from our loss. When something reminds us of those who have gone before us, we still feel the pain and grieve. I was taught to keep going no matter how much it hurts. If we allow ourselves to sink into depression, we disrespect the memory of those we lost. They wouldn't want us to cease to function because of them. As hard as loss is, we must cling to the hope that we will see them again in paradise with God; if we are good enough to receive God's grace, we are assured of this eventuality. There is always hope.

When we learn to deal with the hardest things in life, the easier things get a lot easier too. I was raised a perfectionist; everything had a place, and everything should be in its place. There was a particular way of doing things, and it should always be done that way. A schedule, like a budget, was meant to be kept. I had always been an uptight step-by-step kind of person. Now when I feel frustration creeping in because things were not going according to my plan, I am able to say things like, "Well, *God* doesn't want me to do that right now, so it will have to wait. I am not going to make myself unhappy trying to force something that just isn't going to happen right now anyway."

This lesson is a very important life lesson.

The question is, does living a life that closely follows scripture make that person immune to hardship? No. Not at all. Life still happens, the good and the bad.

When the fight with cancer was over, I didn't know what to do. Then the loneliness set in. I mourned for two years. During this time, my pastor told me, "You may not be ready to hear this. I want you to consider the possibility that God is giving you a chance to do it again, even better. Not that you did anything wrong the first time. With all that you have learned, at your age, you have time to start another relationship."

I wasn't ready to hear that at the time.

Since that time, I have busied myself with my surviving family, my career, and things I enjoy, like writing. I try to stay fit and active. I have made new friends but still, find myself doing things by myself. I know I am not alone; Jesus Christ is with me through it all.

I often think of the poem "Footprints in the sand" by Margaret Fishback Powers.[1] The worst times come at the end of the day. When the work is done, supper has been eaten, the dishes are done, and I wonder what I will do between now and sleep time. That used to be the time when my late wife and I would do something together. We

---

1      https://footprintssandpoem.com/margaret-fishback-powers-version-of-footprints-in-the-sand/

would watch movies, dance to our songs, build puzzles or play games together. The stuff we imagined doing together for the rest of our lives after retirement.

I didn't think it would be any other way. Then I found myself reverting to the feeling of being robbed of thirty years with my soulmate. I felt that anger raise its head deep in my heart. I struggled with it for a long time.

As time went by, the hurt and loss were replaced by the good memories we built together and shared. I started to mingle again, looking for someone to share life with. My sister-in-law asked me, "How do I move on from something like this?"

I told her, "I will always remember your sister fondly. She told me she wanted me to go on and be happy. I will carry this scar for the rest of my life. My courage to try again has to be stronger than my fear of being hurt again."

It hasn't been easy. For a while, I felt like I was cheating on my wife. It has given me the opportunity to be patient with relationships. I pause and reflect on what I feel in my heart. I ask God to lead, guide, and direct me. The desire to share my relationship with God with other people is stronger than it has ever been.

Looking back on my pastor's advice, I now see the wisdom he was sharing with me. Now I feel a compulsion to do more for the kingdom of God. The real-life events I have come through exhibit the power of a scripturally accurate faith. Sometimes it seems like the world and/or the worldly people in it are about to win. Then something unexplainable happens, and life gets better for a season. Other times it seems like life couldn't get any better, and I have to remind myself to stay humble and be a good steward of what God has blessed me with.

The experiences I have to share with fellow believers and those seeking a more accurate scripture-based faith are many and varied. If I can share anything that helps another person in their walk of faith, I would be blessed by sharing it with them.

Let us go back to the question, "Did you know that you go to hell for lying?" It is a commandment; thou shall not lie or bare false witness. If quoting the Bible offends you, those offenses are your demons. I am not sporting a pitchfork!

Believers experience nonbelievers lying to us as a kind of everyday challenge to faith that we face. Those who do not have faith in anything seem to get away with breaking all the rules. That is where I must call out the thought that the devil planted in my mind.

That person is not getting away with anything. They may not have any immediate consequences in this life, but they are subject to the curses for disobedience. Also, they will have eternal consequences when they stand before *God*. There they will have to explain why they said what they said. They will also have to answer for everything they did in life.

Nonbelievers consider themselves free from *God's* judgment. They are not playing for eternity. They have bought into the devil's lie that *God* cannot punish them. Nonbelievers like to say, "You can't judge me." I don't have to; *God* has that covered, "It is written..."

I do not expect nonbelievers to understand. I have experienced nonbelievers do injustice to me. I have prayed for them. Then in *God's* time, I have seen such a person suffer some mishap. I look at the list of curses in Deuteronomy chapter 28. What happened to them falls on that list somewhere. It is all the proof I need. This works for real!

Jesus Christ has been on this field we call the game of life. He has suffered the injustice of the worldly. He told us to obey all of

*God's* laws to the best of our ability. He died a gruesome death to demonstrate we do not need to fear dying for our faith. He promised us unimaginable rewards in heaven. All we must do is be obedient to *God*. Once we put *God* first through our faith, our life experience will improve. The secret is to play for eternity.

Someday we will stand before *God* and give an account for our words and deeds. We should speak and act in this life as we understand Jesus Christ spoke and acted when he was here. The Bible tells us there is no limit to the things we can accomplish for good through faith when we put *God* first.

If you have never heard any of this before, I am glad to bring it to your attention. I pray that *God* will make that seed of faith grow in your mind and heart. That your faith will pay eternal dividends for you. That someday, we will be together in paradise with *God*, where *He* intended us to be.

I pray for all those who deny faith has any benefits. May it be *God's* will that you are saved before it is too late. There is no joy when a soul is lost, only when one is saved.

# Chapter 8

## OBSTACLES TO FAITH

One of the most difficult things for a person of faith is an unbeliever. This is how it goes; the unbeliever doesn't know about Jesus Christ because they do not *want* to know about Him. They do not want to know about Him because there are so many other worldly things that they are focusing on. Those other things are what they care about. They don't care about spiritual eternity, faith, or salvation. The believer cannot make them care about any of it, even though we know that they will pay for it spiritually.

Unbelief is not knowing, not wanting to know, not caring, and not wanting to care. Even though there is a cost for that, the unbeliever does not register the cost. The eternal soul is nothing to them. Faith in the pursuit of salvation is denying oneself the pleasures in life we were all meant to enjoy.

That is the heaviest burden a person of faith carries, knowing a soul will be lost. It is not the believer who changes people's hearts. That is God's work. People who do not believe cannot understand why other people do. Literally, there is no amount of words that can change an unbeliever into a believer. They have free will, and they can choose to believe in whatever they want. Trying to control their free will to suit our beliefs in faith is violating God's law.

"Live wisely among those who are not believers, and make the most of every opportunity. Let your conversation be gracious and attractive so that you will have the right response for everyone" (Colossians 4:5–6, NLT).

61

We disapprove of the sin, not the person committing it. We do not know what they are going through. But we know who does. The God we say we believe in knows all. He sees into the thoughts of every person. He weighs the motives and intentions of each person's heart. In God's time, and for God's purpose, He will change people's minds and hearts.

If we try to force the issue, it is selfish, arrogant, prideful, and counterproductive. We display intolerance for unbelievers. Instead, we need to let our example and the blessings we enjoy speak to the unbeliever in nonverbal communication. We practice our faith for our reasons. Those reasons are not the same as the unbelievers for their nonbelief. We cannot allow ourselves to be discouraged by those who remain in unbelief.

The unbeliever is not a threat to our belief. We can still speak the most eloquent of prayers for all unbelievers in the privacy of our own sanctuaries. God will still hear our prayers. We must recognize our limitations and leave God's work to God.

# Chapter 9

## Oh, God!

### Why Do the Wicked Prosper?

*Lord, you always give me justice when I bring a case before you. So let me bring you this complaint: Why are the wicked so prosperous? Why are evil people so happy? You have planted them, and they have taken root and prospered. Your name is on their lips, but you are far from their hearts.*

Jeremiah 12:1–2 (NLT)

From my experience as an evildoer, I can tell you that looks can be mighty deceiving. This story is completely true. After my debacle with the fiancé and the abortion, I hooked up with an exotic dancer. We lived in sin. One of her coworkers broke up with her fiancé and needed a place to stay. I was then living with two exotic dancers.

We were staying at an apartment complex with three-hundred units. There was an in-ground pool there. Since the girls worked nights, they liked to go out to the pool when they woke up, about two o'clock in the afternoon. Every male in the complex would come by the pool when both girls were sunning themselves.

I was approached by dozens of guys asking me if either girl was single. I was asked if there was going to be any party later. I was asked if the girls were escorts. All the other guys thought I was the luckiest man in the world. Of course, I played it like I was enjoying it.

The truth was those two girls fought like cats and dogs. Everything from sleeping wrong to taking too much time in the bathroom was a continuous argument between the girls. I was the tiebreak in every argument. Somebody was always upset with me.

The only reprieve was they danced at different clubs. Once they were at work, my peace returned. The point is so many other men thought I was living the dream life; they saw me doing well. It didn't matter what the truth was. It is the same way when we see the wicked prospering.

How? God sees all and knows all. Every sin is recorded. Every person will have to answer to God for their thoughts, words, and deeds. The wicked will have their day in court, the Court of the Almighty. No lies will stand before God. In evidence will be the person's own thoughts, motives, and intentions. These will witness and testify against them.

That scares me! I will be in those shoes when it is my turn. I am trying to be good. How will those who are actively pursuing sin fair? We don't see the big picture, but I like to express my belief in the eleventh commandment, "Thou shall not get away with anything!"

We may not see the wicked person suffer. They are very careful to hide it. They want to keep up the image that everything is fine. Which is a lie. The devil is the father of lies. What do we expect from his children? If they are the children of perdition, then they are also heirs to the eternal reward of their father. What do they profit? It is a distraction from our focus on God to worry about the wicked and their deeds.

We shouldn't waste our time second-guessing God. We know the wicked are exercising their God-given free will to do sinful things. We know God will hold them accountable. We should pray for them to find God and seek redemption.

# Chapter 10

## What Is the Unforgivable Sin?

"But the teachers of religious law who had arrived from Jerusalem said, 'He's possessed by Satan, the prince of demons. That's where he gets the power to cast out demons'" (Mark 3:22, NLT).

The leaders and teachers of religious law in the time of Christ were certainly aware of people possessed by demons. It is to their chagrin that they could not perform a successful exorcism. Then along comes Jesus of Nazareth, and He commands the demons to come out, and they obey Him. That seriously discredits the religious leaders and teachers of the law of the time. It also bolsters the street credibility of Jesus. Jesus can do what the leaders and teachers cannot.

To make Jesus look bad and spin the negative impact of that event, the leaders and teachers charged Jesus with being the prince of demons; that is where they say Jesus got His power to cast out demons. This is what those who could not cast out demons from possessed people charged against Jesus Christ.

Jesus goes on to tell us that a house divided cannot stand, so if the prince of demons was casting out demons, that would be a divided house, and it would fall. That made the leaders and teachers look increasingly more foolish.

Then Jesus goes on to tell us that blaspheme of the Holy Spirit is the only unforgivable sin. I reference the unforgivable sin this way: "They repay me evil for good, to the bereavement of my soul" (Psalm 35:12, BSB). And Psalm 109:4–5 (BSB), "In return for my love they accuse me, but I am a man of prayer. They repay me evil for good, and hatred for my love."

This is the transposing of good for evil or overcoming good with evil, which is the unforgivable sin. The leaders and teachers committed blaspheme against the Holy Spirit when they accused Jesus Christ of being the prince of demons.

It is also referenced in the context of a person who comes to know Jesus Christ. This person is baptized, reads the scripture, prays to God, is blessed with the gifts of the Holy Spirit, and enjoys the benefits of their faith. Then that person turns from faith in God. Renounces their belief in God. Begins to live a sinful life, never repenting for the sins they are committing. "But whoever blasphemes against the Holy Spirit will never be forgiven; he is guilty of eternal sin" (Mark 3:29, BSB).

We certainly do not want to come to Jesus Christ and then turn away from Him. That is one reason why I say a person's journey in faith should be a lifelong pursuit.

# Chapter 11

## Lucifer Equals Loser for Sure

For a person new to scripture-based faith they have so much information to absorb and sort through it is hard to make sense of anything. After you know that the human "first estate" was with *God* in paradise forever, the next thing that I find important to know is that the tempter is a loser.

The one who lost his fight against *God* turns his sights on easier prey. He decides to pick on the creation rather than the Creator. The list of Lucifer's fails is extensive. *God* defeated him every time.

*#1 Lucifer loses the battle in heaven and is cast out of heaven.*

> *Then war broke out in heaven. Michael and his angels fought against the dragon, and the dragon and his angels fought back. But he was not strong enough, and they lost their place in heaven. The great dragon was hurled down— that ancient serpent called the devil, or Satan, who leads the whole world astray. He was hurled to the earth, and his angels with him.*

Revelation 12:7–9 (NIV)

*#2 Lucifer kicked out of the Garden of Eden and cursed on earth.*

> *"So, the LORD God said to the serpent: 'Because you have done this, cursed are you above all livestock, and every beast of the field! On your belly will you go, and dust you will eat, all the days of your life'"*

(Genesis 3:14, BSB)

After that, God put enmity between the serpent and the woman and between the seed of the serpent and the seed of the woman forever.

"And I will put enmity between you and the woman, and between your seed and her seed. He will crush your head, and you will strike his heel" (Genesis 3:15, BSB).

People say, "*Hate* is a very strong word." *Enmity* is even stronger. Enmity is a kill-on-sight kind of hatred. That is what the fallen angels have toward humankind, enmity. The war is real.

*#3 Lucifer's success corrupting men undone in the time of Noah with the Flood.*

> *"So the LORD said, 'I will wipe from the face of the earth the human race I have created—and with them the animals, the birds and the creatures that move along the ground— for I regret that I have made them'"*

(Genesis 6:7, NIV)

*#4 Lucifer's success corrupting humans undone at the tower of Babel.*

> *"Come, let Us go down and confuse their language, so that they will not understand one another's speech"*

(Genesis 11:7, BSB)

*#5 Lucifer's success corrupting humans undone at Sodom and Gomorrah.*

> *"Then the LORD rained down burning sulfur on Sodom and Gomorrah—from the LORD out of the heavens"*

(Genesis 19:24, NIV)

*#6 Lucifer unable to break Job.*

*"In all this Job did not sin or charge God with wrong"*

(Job 1:22, BSB)

*#7 Lucifer cannot trick Jesus into sinning once.*

*"Jesus answered, 'It is written: 'Man shall not live on bread alone, but on every word that comes from the mouth of God'"*

(Matthew 4:4, NIV)

*#8 Lucifer cannot trick Jesus into sinning twice.*

*"Jesus replied, 'It is also written: 'Do not put the Lord your God to the test'"*

(Matthew 4:7, BSB)

*#9 Lucifer cannot trick Jesus into sinning three times.*

*"Away from Me, Satan!" Jesus declared. "For it is written: 'Worship the Lord your God and serve Him only'"*

(Matthew 4:10, BSB)

*#10 Jesus beat Lucifer at the cross.*

*"Now since the children have flesh and blood, He too shared in their humanity, so that by His death He might destroy him who holds the power of death, that is, the devil"*

(Hebrews 2:14, BSB)

*#11 Jesus' resurrection confirms the devil's loss.*

*"...Why do you look for the living among the dead? He is not here; He has risen! Remember how He told you while He was still in Galilee: 'The Son of Man must be delivered into the hands of sinful men, and be crucified, and on the third day rise again'"*

(Luke 24:5–7, BSB)

*#12 Jesus' ascension validates the devil's time is limited.*

*"'Men of Galilee,' they said, 'why do you stand here looking into the sky? This same Jesus, who has been taken from you into heaven, will come back in the same way you have seen him go into heaven'"*

(Acts 1:11, NIV)

These are just the twelve most potent examples of Father *God*, Yahweh, Jesus Christ, the only-begotten *Son*, and the *Holy Spirit* overcoming Lucifer and evil. If any other matchup was so one-sided, would we even bother considering the loser a legitimate threat? It would be totally unreasonable to think that such a loser could be a contender.

That is the Holy Trinity; Father *God*, Jesus Christ, and the Holy Spirit have accumulated twelve victories, and Lucifer has zero victories against them! What does the future hold in scripture? It predicts the end of Lucifer's reign of terror. Three hundred scriptural prophecies about Jesus Christ have already come true. These are equally certain.

Jesus' prophesized return in victory.

*and from Jesus Christ, the faithful witness, the firstborn from the dead, and the ruler of the kings of the earth. To Him who loves us and has released us from our sins by His blood, who has made us to be a kingdom, priests to His God and Father—to Him be the glory and power forever and ever! Amen.*

Revelation 1:5–6 (BSB)

Lucifer cast into the lake of fire.

"And the devil who had deceived them was thrown into the lake of fire and sulfur, into which the beast and the false prophet had already been thrown. There they will be tormented day and night forever and ever" (Revelation 20:10, BSB).

Lucifer is 0–12 when fighting *God*. Lucifer is prophesized to die 0–13. Now you know why the number thirteen is considered unlucky! Lucifer/Satan, the devil, a.k.a. the *enemy*, was the most powerful angel in heaven. He persuaded one-third of the host of heaven to follow him into rebellion against God. I believe he did this based on his hatred for God's creation of humankind.

Ever since the failed rebellion, the enemy has set its sights on corrupting the creation and not overtly opposing the Creator. The efforts of the enemy are calculated. There is an intelligent design to their methods and processes. They came from the celestial realm. They know all the policies and procedures that govern heaven. They took them and bent them to service in the infernal realm.

Imagine hell like a skewed vision of the celestial realm. Everything is literally upside down and backward. Instead of championing humankind, here they are zealous about hurting, maiming, crippling, and killing every human possible. They will convince humans to sell their souls for infernal favor, treasure, knowledge, power, a specific partner, fame, and/or anything else a human may desire.

The fallen angels do not care if the human gets what they want; all they care about is conscripting the human's soul. That is the point of contention between light and darkness. Humans as living souls. Before God decided to create humans, he needed to make a habitat suitable for them. At the time of the original idea, the universe was formless and void.

That bleak emptiness is where all the previous creations, the angels in the host of heaven, called home. All business was done there. Then God said, "Let there be light" (Genesis 1:3, BSB), and the entire universe was transformed. Obviously, not every entity that existed before the light was happy with the advent of the light.

Those who hate the light fought the creator of the light and lost. Now they fight to destroy the creation made to dwell in the light. What they are saying is if they cannot have their way, nobody can have anything. They are hell-bent on spoiling everything just to prove their point.

What is their point? That the creation of humankind was a mistake. To prove their point, they must corrupt all of humanity. This is their stock and trade. They are professional, highly motivated, and backed by an industry designed to draw humans into sin. A human's free will is the fulcrum. They leverage toward darkness. Our Creator leverages toward the light. Ultimately, we decide to think, speak, and act as we choose. For good or ill, we make it all happen.

# Chapter 12

## Epiphany

One night in prayer and meditation, I began to dream. In this dream, I was moved into a dorm that looked more like a cave. It was called "*The Lion's Den*." As I walked into the open space for the first time, I felt an uneasy feeling that made me feel nauseous. I saw this center pavilion that looked like a very popular night spot in Austin, Texas. There was nobody in this pavilion. Although it was very tempting to go into this pavilion and partake of the luxurious amenities that were in it, those who called it home would eventually return. I didn't want to have to explain to them why I was trespassing when they came back.

Walking around the perimeter of the cave, I found many tiny caves. They were mostly occupied by other prisoners. I struck up a conversation with one of them in the dream and learned where the vacancy was. I found it; it was a deplorable mess. I spent hours just removing trash from it. Then I had to clean and sanitize it. As I was walking back and forth between my new abode and the guard station to get supplies, I noticed the center pavilion was growing dimmer and smaller. It was also obvious that the perimeter caves were getting brighter and larger.

I fixed my little cave up to be nice as far as prison cells go. I was shaken down by guards repeatedly. They kept thinking I was so slick. They just knew I had something illegal in my cell; they just couldn't find it. This process went on for what seemed like months. The whole time, the center pavilion was unoccupied, getting dimmer and smaller. The outer housing was getting brighter and larger.

While the guards were destroying my nice little cell, I got to know my neighbors. They all seemed to be very senior citizens. They would ask if I would help them with something. I did. It was just simple stuff for me, but a venerable older man couldn't do it himself. I ended up making friends with many of them over time.

Then came the day when the lions returned. It was like a heroes' welcome parade. All the residents in the outer caves peaked out toward the center pavilion. As I saw the first lion enter, I recognized them. One after another, I knew who each one was. They were all my classmates from the high school I graduated from. The captain of the football team, the homecoming queen, the class valedictorian, the doctor's kid, the lawyer's kid, and the professor's kid. One of them was the child of a city council member.

I remember in real life, I transferred to this school when my parents bought a bigger house in a better neighborhood. All these kids were born with silver spoons in their mouths; I was from the poor side of town. That was a distinction that made me unpopular.

After I watched these people make themselves at home in the pavilion, I heard them arguing. The issue was why it had grown smaller and darker. I was the only new arrival since they left. Naturally, it was my fault *their* pavilion had suffered.

The captain of the football team called me out. He blamed me for messing with the pavilion. I told him, "I have never stepped foot in it."

He called me a liar. I told him he could believe whatever he wanted. He started yelling and making threats against me. That is when the neighbors that I had made friends with started showing up. They all vouched for me and said no one ever saw me in the pavilion.

After that, it was the homecoming queen who tried to entice me over to the pavilion. To me, the scenario reeked of a setup. All the guys were mysteriously out of sight and quiet. I just shook my head when she tried to wave me over.

The next thing that happened was loud music started playing, and the guys were acting like it was New Year's Eve. Many of them started waving me over. I noticed they were not inviting anyone else. I saw red flags in that as well.

Finally, it was the lawyer's kid who came over to me, offering me a beer. He said, "Why won't you accept the lion's hospitality?"

In the dream, I answered him with, "I don't want to be lion food."

That caused the lawyer's kid to change into a demon. He started screaming at me. I just laughed and said, "God bless you." The entire center pavilion immediately shrunk and vanished. All the lions went with it. All the prisoners in the caves along the wall of the large chamber cheered. My next-door neighbor came out and shook my hand. "Wisdom is power," he told me.

At this point, I wake up from the dream. It impresses me how the environment changes in this dream. I am being a good steward of what I have, and it grows in size and becomes more luminous. The abode of the lions becomes dimmer and shrinks. I have to resist the temptation to engage in lecherous carousing and debauchery to expose the true nature of the lions. The fellow prisoners in the small caves around the perimeter all have an air about them like old-world prophets. There I am, defying the lions at every turn. Oppose the enemy boldly, and he will flee (James 4:7).

# Chapter 13

## A STRONG SPIRITUAL FAITH

What is heaven? What is it you see in your imagination when you think of being in heaven? What is the place that Jesus has gone to prepare for us? What will it be like to be there?

Some people envision the Garden of Eden, some a magnificent mansion on a hilltop, and others see singing praises to God surrounded by angels. I personally think heaven will be the ability to visit anywhere in the cosmos as a spirit to see and appreciate all the things that God has made.

Whatever your version of heaven is, that is the reward we seek for exercising our free will to be obedient to scripture. Shouldn't we have a clear picture in our mind of what that reward is? That image in your mind is between you and God. That vision is the reason you exercise your free will to think, speak, and act in accordance with scripture. More than that, it is our adherence to scriptural direction for our behavior out of our love for and desire to serve the one who created us.

I hear people talking about heaven. I hear people say, "I am a good person; I know I am going to heaven. I believe in Jesus Christ as my Lord and Savior." Good for you, where will you be? Can you describe it to me? Some people answer that heaven is a place with streets of gold and it sits beside the crystal sea. That would be the new Jerusalem that comes with Jesus at the Second Coming. When I say that, those who would answer me seem to be in deep thought or a state of confusion.

Just believing in Him is not enough. The enemy wants people to believe it is that easy to make his job easier. Anyone can think they are saved by the grace of God, but what does God think about that? Depends on your thoughts, words, and deeds. Are they obedient or not?

There are over six hundred laws in the Bible. This includes the Ten Commandments and many other laws, statutes, and ordinances. There were at least sixty prophets in the Old Testament. When Jesus Christ is speaking in Matthew 5:17, He tells us that He did not come to abolish the laws and prophets but to fulfill them.

Contrary to the sentiment that simple belief in Jesus Christ is all a person needs to be saved, here in Matthew, Jesus is saying, "My existence validates everything that has come before Me."

That means we are still subject to the six hundred laws and the lessons taught by the sixty prophets. This would be the structure for a Scripture-based code of conduct. We have the laws and the lessons of the prophets to guide us.

Then Jesus Christ appears. His example fulfills the scriptural laws and the lessons given to us by the prophets. There is an element of hindsight given to us. Before Jesus Christ, the old laws and prophets of old only pointed to some future person.

Those who studied the laws and prophetic teachings available at that time hoped for something other than what they saw in Jesus Christ. Not until Matthew 6:16–17 do we find out just how rare the accurate human understanding of the existing scripture really was.

If only one of the twelve disciples knew who Jesus Christ really was, how does that bode for us today? For over two thousand years, the enemy of God has been trying to deceive the whole world. Even though we certainly know Jesus Christ, many people have been erroneously taught that all they need to be saved is faith that Jesus was a real person; He lived, was crucified, and rose on the third day.

It is very important to our faith to understand that this happened. The problem comes when people think that they can speak and act in any way and still be saved because of their faith in the person of Jesus Christ. Understand this, scripture tells us the good things happen to people who do good, and bad things happen to people who do bad (Romans 2:6–8). God will bless those who do good and punish those who do bad. We are to he happy when God chastises us because we can learn, grow, and change to be more pleasing to God (Job 5:17).

We know what is good: obedience to the law and practicing the lessons taught by the prophets. We also know what is bad: disobedience to the law and not practicing the lessons taught by the prophets.

I am neither increased by anyone who accepts this nor decreased by anyone who refuses it. The truth will be the same no matter how it is received or rejected.

What every person must decide for themselves, between their self and God, is, "Do I want to enjoy God's pleasure or suffer His wrath?"

To be blessed, we must be obedient. Obedient to what? The six hundred plus laws and over sixty prophets who taught us their lessons. If we go only by, "Jesus is a friend of mine," and we break just one law of the six hundred, we are guilty of breaking the whole law. Jesus will look at you and say, "Have you repented for your sins?" If we have not repented, we cannot be forgiven. If we are unforgiven, we cannot be saved.

Therein is the lie of the enemy when we hear, "All you need to be saved is faith in Jesus Christ."

Lucifer/Satan wants you to believe that. It makes his job so much easier. We parade around thinking we're saved *while* speeding through a yellow light, fudging on our taxes or tithes, looking the other way when the homeless need our help; you understand what I am saying. Any small infraction makes us guilty as a cold-blooded murderer. Guilty of violating the whole system of law.

All Lucifer/Satan does is point us out to God and accuse us of wrongdoing. How easy is that? Another soul going to hell.

We may try to argue, "I know Jesus; it is all good."

God will ask us, "Have you made atonements for all your sins?"

We will respond, "Jesus paid the price for all my sins."

God will say to us, "Jesus paid for the sins you confessed to Him. The rest are still outstanding on your account."

We will stand convicted before God while Lucifer/Satan does a little happy dance. The enemy of God will say to us, "You know I am the father of lies, right?"

We may cry, "It's not fair; no one told me about this obedience to the law and prophet's stuff."

God will tell us, "My Word has been preached in every nation on earth. Bibles are the most abundant publication on earth. There are church buildings everywhere. My message is broadcast on radio and television 24/7/365. You can find Me on the internet anytime. My app is available on your mobile device. You should have tried to know Me better. How is it fair to Me that you didn't love Me enough to find out what I expected of you so you could be reconciled to Me? You missed the opportunity to save your life; it is a natural consequence of your exercise of the free will I gave you. You can choose to believe a lie if you want to. That does not exonerate you from the responsibility of being a good steward (1 Peter 4:10). My word encourages you to test the spirits (1 John 4:1). If you knew My Son, you would see the light (2 Corinthians

6:14). While you stand in the shadow of guilt, I cannot ransom you."

On the flip side of this scenario, if we have been good stewards, faithfully tested the spirits, and sought forgiveness every day for our sins, knowing Jesus Christ will ransom us from the enemy of God. This battle is for eternity. The enemy of God is patient. We must be persistent in our faith.

If we believe in our eternal soul and that our life in the physical world can make or break our path to this eternal paradise, shouldn't we know what is expected of us? Who determines these expectations? How do we know when we have accomplished these expectations?

I say yes, we should know what is expected of us. God is the author of scripture and thus what is expected of us. Study of scripture must be a lifelong pursuit. I hear people say that they read the bible once, a long time ago. The Lord's Prayer asks God for our daily bread. Jesus said, "Man does not live by bread alone but by every word that comes from the mouth of God." (Matthew 4:4, BSB).

Scripture is soul food; we need to feed our souls every day. The Bible is the only book I have read more than once and got something different out of it each time I have read it. No other book has done that for me. That is why the Bible is special to me.

Modern life leaves little leisure time for studying scripture and meditating on what it means to us. Instead of reading ourselves, we listen to preachers give sermons or watch YouTube videos of sermons, but we are passive in that capacity. God wants us to actively seek Him.

Many self-help and motivational works purport to increase the readers' success and satisfaction with life. There may be certain validity to such works, but they are imagined by people. Scripture is God's word. The scriptures are intended to guide the creation to what the Creator has in store for us. That is the best source of information for us.

Works published by people promise big results in little time with specified effort. God tells us to search for wisdom as if seeking fine treasure. Treasure hunters spend many hours tracking down leads and searching out what the clues mean. Blind luck seems to have more to do with finding treasure than concrete evidence. That can be very confusing.

We know we have attained a level of success with our understanding of scripture when we can apply what it teaches us to our daily lives and recognize a benefit from doing so.

The confusion in the world today led me to search scripture for how I should act in my scriptural walk. I started out reading a chapter from the Old and New Testaments every day. When I finished either, I would start over again. Now I just read from Genesis to Revelation and start over. I also like to read a chapter of Proverbs every day; there are thirty-one chapters in Proverbs, so every day of the month is a different chapter. I also read Psalms every day. There are one-hundred-fifty of them, so that works out to reading five every day for a thirty-day month.

As important as it is to obey the Ten Commandments, there are many more laws, statutes, and ordinances in scripture. We must obey those as well. That is a lot to consider. What is our motivation? Or what should our motivation be?

Just following the letter of the law is not enough. Jesus told the Pharisees this when He walked our earth. God knows our thoughts, hears every word we speak, and sees every act we do. Our intent for what we think, say, and do is also open for inspection before God.

Early in my Christian walk, I tried to get by with shortcuts. Then I realized the Israelites had already tried that. They worshiped Baal, grew groves of trees on hilltops, and burned incense to Baal in those groves. Those Israelites were punished, and the next generation was given the free will to decide for themselves to be obedient to scripture or not.

"And they did that which was evil in the sight of the Lord" is a popular verse in the Old Testament. What is the consequence of doing evil? Some people ask, "Why do evil people prosper?" The price God laid upon sinners is twofold.

First are the blessings for obedience and curses for disobedience. What is obedience? We are told to not let the sun go down on our sin (Ephesians 4:26). That means every day, we must ask for forgiveness for what we did wrong. The things we know we did wrong and the things we don't believe are wrong, just to be safe. The Lord is faithful to forgive if we ask in Jesus' name (1 John 1:9).

What is disobedience? Doing what we know is wrong and refusing to seek forgiveness. (Romans 1:21–32).

Second is eternal suffering for those whose name is not found in the Lamb's book of life. (Revelation 20:15).

When I found the curses pronounced against humankind for disobedience, I saw the consequences for sin in our physical life. I felt motivated to be right with God more than ever before.

There are also blessings pronounced by God for people who are obedient to scripture. I saw the value in being obedient to obtain blessings in my physical life. The side effect is I would be increasing my chances of getting into paradise for eternity.

The greatest gift one person can give to another is a more accurate understanding of God, scripture, and how to preserve one's own eternal soul. I am trying to share this gift with my readers.

What exactly are the curses that God pronounced against humankind? How do we be obedient to God and obtain His blessings upon us? What does winning this game look like?

I really want *us* to be on a winning team. I want us to be champions for our eternal lives. We are talking about the outward expression of our inner faith. How we think, speak, and act in our everyday life is our walk in faith. Walk with me so the sound of our steps strikes fear in the enemy.

When we endeavor to make a faith change in our lives and take positive steps toward that purpose, we run into obstacles. I have heard people say that their life was fine before they started getting into faith. Many of them told me, "As soon as I accepted Jesus Christ as my Lord and Savior, things started going wrong."

That is proof the devil is active in the world. If you are not declared to Jesus, you will share the same fate as the devil. *God* will not accept what He calls "lukewarm" followers (Revelation 3:16). The devil knows this. If you are not saved, you are already considered to be on the devil's side by default.

I recognize people new to faith have significant challenges to overcome. The devil knows the obstacles that work best. Careful research in the Bible uncovers scripture that helps us enjoy a successful faith with the least amount of drama, setbacks, and dismay. It takes a long time to study up and learn these things. Often sifting and winnowing are required between different chapters, various books, and even other translations. Sometimes a concordance is necessary to look up the keywords in a scripture and see what other possible meanings they could have. It is work, it takes time, and once you learn it, it cannot be taken away from you.

Life still happens. A person of faith is not immune to that. They just have a source of comfort that is part of their faith. Jesus Christ suffered when He was here. He said He would never leave us or forsake us. He didn't promise us a trouble-free life.

Many scriptures teach us how to be faithful. Knowing these scriptures and applying their lessons in your life can help you improve your life experience.

It helps to know what you are up against. The weapons, strategies, and tactics of the enemy of humanity. It is empowering to know that we were all meant for better. Knowing the proper scriptural steps to take will help people get there.

Common attacks of Satan include doubt, fear, distraction, and selfish pursuits. People new to faith are not taught to be prepared for such attacks. When a person declares themselves for Jesus Christ, they are taking sides in a very old spiritual war. Jesus won the war for us, but many battles still rage. In fact, the devil is still battling for every human soul on earth. The devil wants to play spoiler for us. He knows his fate is sealed. He doesn't want to be alone in his punishment. Every human is his target.

There are a great many spiritual protections in scripture. Once we learn them and apply them in our faith, the devil has a tougher time spoiling us. We are not invincible, but *God* is. The scriptures are *God's* words to us. The Holy Bible is the faithful person's "tactical strategy guide for dealing with spiritual attacks of the devil."

When a person first steps into faith, it is very similar to starting to learn a new game, sport, or profession. If you have never done it before, you do not know all the rules, the historical lessons, the places, and people that make up the history. Learning these things take time, a lot of it. I encourage everyone to see their walk of faith as a lifelong pursuit.

Our reality is the world, and worldly people see people of faith as weak or gullible. They often mistake our kindness for weakness.

They cannot perceive God working in our lives or in the world. For them, it must be tangible to exist. That precludes the possibility of them having faith in anything. Such people are fond of saying, "I will believe it when I see it." The problem is one cannot see God working until they believe God exists and is working. It is a freewill choice.

I hope this work helps all people of faith, beginners, the intermediate, and old pros, to be better prepared to give a scriptural answer when we are attacked spiritually (1 Peter 3:15). For all scripture is fit for reproof (2 Timothy 3:16). In my own words, the Bible says you go to hell for lying. It is a commandment, do not lie. Those who lie are facing eternal consequences for it. Maybe nothing happens to the liar in this life. People of faith know how to deal with that as well.

Learning this is a process. I had a good start in life. Made many mistakes and found rock bottom. From being there, I turned my life over to Christ in scripture-based faith. Now I am doing better than I ever thought possible.

When I first began this journey in 1994, I had a great many questions. I made a friend who knew the scriptures and helped me find answers there. Every person is different. The way each of us perceives our world and the events we experience is unique to each person. Where you are in your life matters as well. Are you under twenty-one? A parent? Over fifty? These things matter when reading scripture and building your faith.

I consider the Bible the playbook for life. You don't have to memorize the whole playbook. It is more advantageous to you to know how to use the "playbook" as a reference material. Many apps these days allow new believers to search the scriptures for specific topics.

If you never picked up a Bible before, such apps would tell you what book, chapter, and verse of the Bible your topic is discussed in. You can click on the link to that reference and be taken straight to the scripture. Often there is more than one reference for any specific topic.

The playbook is not an exercise in memorization. It describes a way of playing the game that leads to victory. Applying the principles given in the playbook to your everyday life is living a winning life in faith. The championship of faith is making it to heaven.

What if I don't get along with the coach? The coach is in the business of winning. If the coach wants you to do things differently than you have been, you can believe there is a good reason for it. (*God*, Jesus Christ, and the Holy Spirit are the coaches, and the Holy Bible is the playbook.)

The reality is you will get out of it no more than you put into it. If you give it your all, there is no limit to the success you can achieve. God wants us to live a life with greater abundance (John 10:10, KJV). God says, "See if I will not open the windows of heaven and pour out for you blessing without measure" (Malachi 3:10, BSB).

What kind of knowledge, skill, and effort does it take to overcome every challenge to your spiritual success? What are the unknowns that you must be prepared to address along the way?

Life is tough. We must navigate many challenges every day. There are times that it seems like no one is on our side. Often our problems grow out of the things we don't know. How are we supposed to do better if we don't know; that we don't know something?

For this writing, the game I speak of is the game of life. When we play a game, we all desire to do well. We crave success. Any bit of recognition inspires us to try even harder. Going through struggles, we try to minimize our pain, shame, and loss. We believe things have got to get better. Sometimes it takes a while for that to happen. While we keep hope, we can bare many pains.

It takes a while to figure out what is going wrong when you don't know that not knowing something is causing you to fail. You do all you can to make the experience more pleasant. You ask people who have been through it before how they did it. You try to put into practice what worked for others before you. The fact remains that you keep ending up on the short end of almost every deal.

You have no idea what is about to unfold before your eyes. You cannot comprehend the depth of the evil that is about to be set loose upon you. It just seems like no matter what you do to make things better; things just keep getting worse. There is no one to stand up for what is right or true. The whole world sees it and smiles when it says with venomous apathy, "Better you than me." Well, I can't take that! I won't let that be part of my reality. How do I get past the world and the worldly people in it?

It takes knowing what you have been missing. I was missing it for a lot of my life. I was raised Catholic. I was baptized as a baby, went to catechism as I grew up, and took communion at a young age. I went to church. My family prayed every day. My family watched all the religious movies around Christmas and Easter. All those things worked together to form my impression of *God*, religion, and life.

I thought I had a pretty good handle on right and wrong. I believed I was a good person. I considered most people in the world to be good people. As I grew up, I began to learn that everything I was taught was not an accurate reflection of the real world.

The secret is in this scripture, "For wide is the gate and broad is the way that leads to destruction, and many enter through it" (Matthew 7:13, NIV). That means God already knows the human exercise of free will will lead to many ending up in destruction. I rationalize it as a natural consequence of free will. God does not stand over His creation and direct traffic. There are no bolts of lightning for people who willfully do wrong. If people think they can get away with something, they will try to do so. I say there is an eleventh commandment, "Thou shalt not get away with anything." God knows all, sees all, and is everywhere at all times. Nothing can be hidden from Him.

To check my logic, reference Matthew 7:14 (BSB), "Small is the gate and narrow the way that leads to life, and only a few find it." That means that God already knows the human exercise of free will leads to few people finding life. I rationalize this as the *other* consequence for the human exercise of free will. God knows it is a challenge for his creation to find success. The reward is eternal happiness in heaven with God. That means we must work harder to succeed.

Often when inspired by the Holy Spirit in earnest faith, we are struggling with the world and worldly people in it. At times like this, we give it all to God and ask Him to make the changes He knows are best for the world. It is at this time we are given a spiritual glimpse of the way the world should look.

When we see this spiritual glimpse, the physical world appears upside down and backward from it. This is a divine blessing! The devil has deceived the world. Worldly existence reflects the spiritual one. As with any reflection in a mirror, the world reflects heaven backward in the devil's mirror. It is also reflecting up what is seen from below.

*The wicked will not rule the land of the godly, for then the godly might be tempted to do wrong. O LORD, do good to those who are good, whose hearts are in tune with you. But banish those who turn to crooked ways, O LORD. Take them away with those who do evil.*

Psalm 125:3–5 (NLT)

When I see people of faith struggling with this spiritual vision from the divine and the physical appearance from the devil, I feel moved in the spirit to persuade them to reconcile what they are seeing, both spiritually and physically. To achieve this, I often ask people who are struggling with their situation in life, "Are you doing what you are because you want to? Or are you just doing what you think is expected of you?"

The answer to that question is very important. It brings a load of reality into the person's thought process. I already know that very few people are fortunate enough to do just what they want to. Most people live their life just getting by while trying to live up to the expectations they place on themselves.

When I noticed this phenomenon, I tried it against the scriptures. How does any person "put on themselves" expectations? Nobody goes out to deliberately lose. Even those who self-sabotage do not know that they are doing it in the moment it happens. It is possible to do everything right and still get beat.

In our daily life, we take on expectations aimed at bringing us the largest amount of the most potent kind of happiness we can imagine. It starts out when we see something we want. We decide to conditionally change our behavior long enough to get that something in our lives.

People are doing all they know how to get what they want. We subliminally program ourselves to do what we need to so we can accumulate the things we want. Those are the expectations we place on ourselves. Where do such expectations come from? Our religion? Our faith?

There is a sentiment among corporate boss types that workers under stress perform better. I don't believe that. What I believe is that some people will procrastinate until they have no choice but to get after their assignment. I see this as another self-imposed detriment. The person procrastinating knows what they need to do. They simply exercise their free will to put it off as long as possible.

To me, that is setting up self for failure. If you run into unexpected problems or underestimate the challenge or the time it takes, your stress will explode. I would rather start early, give a strong effort from the start, and look strong at a successful finish.

I think our walk in faith should be approached the same way. Why stress about your relationship with God? Make Him your everyday friend by reading His word every day and applying it in your life daily. It takes a sustained effort over time. We are encouraged to: "For this very reason, make every effort to add to your faith virtue; and to virtue, knowledge; and to knowledge, self-control; and to self-control, perseverance; and to perseverance, godliness; and to godliness, brotherly kindness; and to brotherly kindness, love" (2 Peter 1:5–7, BSB).

The reason we are encouraged to do these things is to become effective and productive disciples of Scripture. "For if you possess these qualities and continue to grow in them, they will keep you from being ineffective and unproductive in your knowledge of our Lord Jesus Christ" (2 Peter 1:8, BSB).

This means that there is an inherent accountability for good stewardship in our faith to scripture and God when we profess to love our Creator. God professes His jealousy over us. I take that to mean we should also be jealous of our relationship with God. Let nothing come between us!

> *Son of man, I have made you a watchman for the house of Israel. Whenever you hear a word from My mouth, give them a warning from Me. If I say to the wicked man, 'You will surely die,' but you do not warn him or speak out to warn him from his wicked way to save his life, that wicked man will die in his iniquity, and I will hold you responsible for his blood.*

> Ezekiel 3:17–18 (BSB)

I understand this to mean that as a disciple of Scripture, I am in tune with a more accurate understanding of scripture than the layman. I know God wants to save every soul possible. If I am a good steward, I have the desire in my heart to help God save souls. Whether I know it or not, if I accept it or not, God is going to hold me responsible for warning the wicked person about what they are risking by committing wickedness.

As long as I do my job in good faith, exercise due diligence, and give all the praise, honor, glory, and thanks to God, I do not have to save every person who is thinking, speaking, and/or doing wickedness. Every person still has free will. That cannot be infringed. "But if you warn a wicked man and he does not turn from his wickedness and his wicked way, he will die in his iniquity, but you will have saved yourself" (Ezekiel 3:19, BSB).

This tells me that my job is complete at the point I express the truth to the person who is lost. I can tell you from personal experience that it is grievous to reach out with good intentions and be rebuffed.

Worldly people cannot see what people of faith can. It is that simple. No matter what a believer says to convince a nonbeliever, it goes nowhere. Only God can change a person's heart. A good disciple of Scripture knows and accepts this limitation.

> *Now if a righteous man turns from his righteousness and commits iniquity, and I put a stumbling block before him, he will die. If you did not warn him, he will die in his sin, and the righteous acts he did will not be remembered. And I will hold you responsible for his blood.*

Ezekiel 3:20 (BSB)

This is a situation of someone who was walking in the light and strayed off the path. The disciple of Scripture can see them getting into trouble. The disciple may think it is none of their business. God tells us that it is our business, and we must act. God will hold us responsible if we watch a fellow believer wander into the darkness and do nothing to help them.

"But if you warn the righteous man not to sin, and he does not sin, he will indeed live because he heeded your warning, and you will have saved yourself" (Ezekiel 3:21, BSB).

I understand this to mean when you tell someone, "Keep fighting the good fight," you have encouraged them in faith, and that is good.

I have heard people say things like, "I prayed for God to tell me what I should do. I haven't seen any angels or heard any voice from heaven telling me what to do. I guess I don't have a part in God's plan." This is like asking God for a sign that He is real before you will do what scripture says you should.

If a person has not confessed their sins to God, asked for forgiveness, and been forgiven, God does not hear that person's prayers. It is our responsibility to seek what God expects of us. He tells us to knock, and it will be opened, seek, and we shall find (Matthew 7:7, Luke 11:9). "But seek first the kingdom of God and His righteousness, and all these things will be added unto you" (Matthew 6:33, BSB).

I cannot think of a worse situation than trying to share the greatest gift I have ever received with another person, and they won't accept it. I think ahead to the day when *if I am blessed enough* to receive *God's* grace, I am admitted to heaven, who will be there and who will not? I will know those I do not see there are in the other place. The place of much wailing and gnashing of teeth. (Matthew 8:12, 13:42, 13:50, 22:13, 24:51, 25:30; Luke 13:28.)

There is no glory in any sinner being lost, only when one is redeemed (Luke 15:7). I very strongly encourage anyone who will receive this to take it to the heart of all your hearts and make it your daily mission to draw closer to God, and He will draw closer to you. (James 4:8).

# Chapter 14

## FACING THE ENEMY

Now that we know Lucifer is a loser, why is it then that so many people fall for luciferin tricks?

Maybe they are too focused on the loser's game and not focused enough on *God's* game. The Bible tells us to "seek first the kingdom of God and His righteousness, and all these things will be added unto you" (Matthew 6:33, BSB).

What things will be added unto you? "Therefore do not worry, saying, 'What shall we eat?' or 'What shall we drink?' or 'What shall we wear?' For the pagans strive after all these things, and your Heavenly Father knows that you need them. What then is the Kingdom of GOD?" (Matthew 6:31–32, BSB)

"And when he was demanded of the Pharisees, when the kingdom of God should come, he answered them and said, The kingdom of God cometh not with observation: Neither shall they say, Lo here! or, lo there! for, behold, the kingdom of God is within you" (Luke 17:20–21, KJV).

"so that the righteous standard of the law might be fulfilled in us, who do not walk according to the flesh but according to the Spirit" (Romans 8:4, BSB).

In my own words, I describe it this way:

The kingdom of *God* is that small yet persistent voice in your mind that tells you what you know you should do. It combines with that burning feeling in your heart when you feel shame or the swelling feeling in your heart from feelings of joy. It is the shiver down your spine in certain circumstances. It is the hair raising on your arms or the back of your neck. The goosebumps that cover our skin when something unexplainable happens. The object of faith is to embrace those feelings and let them be the major compass and direction finder in your life, not to close them off and ignore them.

*God's* blessing to us is letting all that *God* has bestowed upon us flow through us to our fellow brothers and sisters in Christ Jesus. We are to be conduits sharing with others what *God* has shared with us. In the end, all things belong to *God.* The more freely we give, the more freely we are given. It becomes a matter of our good stewardship paying it forward. As we are tending to *God's* blessings flowing through us to those around us, we are also blessed.

Many people relate this definition to the tithe. Before they committed to giving ten percent to *God*, they had trouble making ends meet. Once they were giving their ten percent regularly, the financial situation worked itself out.

This is not simply about the tithe. It is about all the facets of biblically correct living. I committed myself to *God* and *His* Word in 1994. I began by telling myself that if I found something in the Bible that I needed to change in my life, I would make that change.

Later in 1999, I found myself witnessing to people. I explained to them that I live my life the way I do because I am applying what I know the Bible says I should do in my life. *(Not what I think is expected of me.)* If you can show me something in the Bible that I am not doing right biblically, I will change my ways.

I have had to make little tweaks to my life every so often, but the more I am living in tune with the Bible, the better my life has become.

The more I smile, the more smiles I get. The more laughter I share, the greater my joy. The more work effort I lend to others without the expectation of payment, the more I and those around me accomplish for the greater good.

I have seen it change lives in many ways over the past twenty-five years. I believe it is the greatest gift one human can share with another. A relationship with *God*, the way *God* intended for us to live. These are not my rules; they are all *God's* rules, and they are open to all of humankind.

By these rules of *God*, there are only two kinds of people on earth. There are those people who believe in Jesus Christ as their Lord and Savior, and there are those who do not believe in Jesus Christ as their Lord and Savior.

At this point, I must distinguish between three types of human perceptions of faith:

One perception is accepting Jesus Christ as your personal Lord and Savior (Christians). A second perception is not accepting Jesus Christ as Lord and Savior (non-Christians). The third perception is hating Jesus Christ and all things Christian (anti-Christians).

Non-Christians do not pursue the active use of carefully crafted words to try and pick holes in Scripture or faith in Jesus Christ. They are too busy seeking after the things they want in life. Non-Christians do not act in ways to prevent Christians from expressing their faith in word or deed. Again, they are consumed with other pursuits.

The anti-Christian, however, is ever on an anti-Christian agenda. They always have a formula of words ready to cast doubt on Christian beliefs. They are filing lawsuits to prevent the free expression of the Christian religion. These anti-Christians are the reason I decided to write this manuscript.

Anti-Christians say, "You can't judge me." The truth is, I don't have to; God already has. "It is written," if an anti-Christian comes at a Christian, most Christians tend to avoid conflict. That is what is causing our faith crisis in this country. We are to be "prepared to give an answer" (1 Peter 3:15, KJV). If an anti-Christian is offended by my expression of my faith, I welcome them to the offended club. I am as offended by their disbelief as they are by my belief. I will stand my ground. The anti-Christian's feeling offended is rooted in the vice of pride. They want things their way, and anything that contradicts "their way" offends them. They have no sense of fairness nor any willingness to compromise. With them, it is an all-or-nothing campaign. That is a demonstration of prejudice. My constitutional right to freedom of religion means—"don't worry about my faith." If you don't like it, you don't have to participate. At the same time, the anti-Christians hatred for my faith has no force greater than my love for it.

Politicians funded by anti-Christians like to solve the religion problem by offering two equally unpalatable choices. This is a classic no-win scenario. The Christian can shut up and go away, or the Christian and be quiet somewhere else. Sorry, I don't like either choice, and I am going to stand my ground.

Once the anti-Christian has exposed themselves as such, it is a simple matter of our rights being equal to each other's. In the context of a scripturally accurate faith, there is no law against the fruit of the spirit. There are laws against people committing violence, making terrorist threats, deliberately misrepresenting historical facts, revising the true accounts to make them false, slander, liable, and defamation of character, as well as vandalism, stalking, and cybercrimes.

Only together, through faith, Scripture, prayer, and being bold Christians in word and deed, can we offset the work of anti-Christians. Anti-Christians know the scriptures at least as well as most Christians. They like to quote scriptures such as "turn the other cheek" and "care for your enemy" while engaged in an aggressive anti-Christian campaign.

With those distinctions made, it is not the mission of Christianity to become extinct. We are to continue in our faith, teach our children and others the faith, and spread the faith throughout the whole world. We cannot do that by remaining silent and taking no action to resist the anti-Christian agenda.

When we deal with our fellow brothers and sisters in Christ Jesus, those are the people we deal with as if they have the most favored status on earth. The Bible also tells us, "Do not be unequally yoked with unbelievers" (2 Corinthians 6:14, ESV). (See also Galatians 6:10.)

The way I have lived my life over the past twenty-five years is I give people, in general, a fair chance to prove themselves as Christians, nonbelievers, or anti-Christians. How do I do that?

The Bible tells us, "By their fruit you will recognize them" (Matthew 7:20, BSB). We have a common saying, "Actions speak louder than words." This is that saying in action. Any person can say anything. What they do, however, is unique to them. Even if they do what a lot of other people are doing, they are unique in the way they do it.

This is not any kind of prejudice or profiling or even insult. It is factual observation of a person's demonstrated behavior. It is not my list of actions that is used to compare whether a person is acting like a Christian or not; it is *God's* Word, the Bible, that delineates the types of behavior that either qualify humans as Christians or disqualify them as Christians (Romans 12:2).

When you know how biblically correct Christian living is supposed to look according to the scriptures, then you can "know them by their works."

Another method *God* provided all humans in *His* Word, the Bible, for all humans to recognize believers in Christ from the nonbelievers is the blessings and cursings. Humans were cursed many times for their failure to follow *God's* rules.

Adam and Eve sinned in the Garden of Eden and brought upon the human race the Adamic curses.

After the Israelites were freed from bondage in Egypt, they made a golden calf and worshiped it. That brought upon humans the curses of disobedience. Knowing what these Adamic curses and the curses of disobedience are, *God*-fearing Christians who read the Bible and pray to *God* regularly can see in their own lives and the lives of other people whether they are blessed or cursed. Some people seem to have problems, but they just keep going and enjoying life.

Other people seem to have a steady train of misfortune plaguing them. It can be difficult to discern if a person is a nonbeliever or a believer going through a trial or experiencing a period of enemy attack. Even Jesus Christ, when He walked this earth, had His "life happening" issues, like all humans do today.

If there is ever a lingering doubt about the truth of a person's faith convictions, you can simply ask them, "Do you believe in Jesus Christ as your personal Lord and Savior?" If they say yes and are trying to deceive you, the wrath of *God* will be upon them.

It is also important to pray, especially for discernment, when investigating such things. *God* could be using you to convert a nonbeliever to the faith. *God* could be putting two believers together so they can accomplish even more for the glory of *God*!

In this life, there are no certain determining factors. We can combine what we see and hear with other Christian tools of faith to help identify if a person is a true believer or a wolf in sheep's clothing.

Sometimes a person's language is enough to tell. Other times, it is a matter of working the steps from what cause led to what effect. We add to that what action led to a certain reaction.

Then we have to apply, "What would a person's motive or intent be to derive that certain result?" One step farther is, "Who would want it that way and why?" Most of the time, when dealing with worldly people, it is about the money. Follow the money to see where it ends up.

When we are armed with all those answers and the guidance we find in the Bible, *God* makes the answers clear to us. Back to that little voice in our mind that seems to know stuff we just didn't expect. That feeling in your heart. Those chills up and down your spine. The hair standing up on your arms or the back of your neck. All are indications we should pay attention to when trying to identify friend from foe.

It has been my experience that anti-Christians are the puppets of the devil. Like their master, if they are strongly opposed, they will flee. Be prepared to give an answer, a sound scriptural answer, start with, "It is written," and yes, the constitution and other laws are written as well.

# Chapter 15

## WHAT WE ARE UP AGAINST

The original host of heaven, before the war in heaven, was infinite, innumerable, beyond measure. Lucifer convinced one-third of that number to follow him. Now, Lucifer, the evil one, is the ruler of this worldly system of things. As such, he commands one-third of infinite, innumerable, beyond measure in his army of darkness.

It also means that the host of heaven is still twice that big! I want my readers to remember this fact. For every demon that attacks a person, there are two angles available to fight it. For every kind of evil, there are two kinds of holy to fight it. We can call upon the name of Jesus Christ to send us warring angels to protect us from each demon.

"No temptation has seized you except what is common to man. And God is faithful; He will not let you be tempted beyond what you can bear. But when you are tempted, He will also provide an escape, so that you can stand up under it" (1 Corinthians 10:13, BSB).

I imagine the evil one has set up his army of darkness very intelligently. The forces are aligned against us to their most advantageous. The enemy certainly looks for mismatches to exploit. Any tendencies we exhibit are noticed, and the enemy calculates how to use them against us. For them, it is as real as it gets.

The fallen angels were once in heaven. They knew God. They picked a fight and lost. Now they know heaven will never take them back. God has sentenced them to eternity in the lake of fire. God's creation of humankind is the only thing that they can defeat. They defeat humans by tricking us into sin. We have free will. We know right from wrong. We are not perfect, but we can be forgiven.

The fallen angels condemned to hell cannot be forgiven. They know this. They do not want to be alone when the suffering starts.

Since the creation of humankind, the evil one has studied us. He knows human history better than any human. This enemy of ours has lived through human history. In the enemy's living memory, they can remember the day Adam was created. They also remember every generation, every nation, and every tongue that humans have made.

The entire time, the enmity between the seed of Eve and the seed of the serpent has kept us at war. Enmity is a severe, intense, unquenchable hatred. I call it a "kill on sight" kind of hatred. It is why people hate snakes and kill them on sight; that is worse than hate; it is enmity. I hate spiders and will kill most of them I find in my house. Occasionally, I will catch a spider and let it go outside. I do not have enmity for spiders; I am just lazy. It is easier to kill them with a paper towel and flush it down the toilet than it is to catch them and take them outside.

The evil one is motivated by his own sealed fate. Ever heard the saying, "You cannot bargain with a dead man"? Every soldier in the army of darkness is condemned by God to die. They have nothing to gain or lose by corrupting human souls.

The only thing that matters is the more human souls they corrupt, the better they can hate themselves with a clear conscious. Yes, they failed to win the war in heaven, but they will corrupt many human souls that God made (Matthew 7:13–14). The evil ones may think that they will be tormenting the human souls they corrupted, but they too will be tormented. Hell is the place of much wailing and gnashing of teeth.

Imagine if you were a fallen angel and you knew for sure that you were going to die, and you believed that corrupting human souls would ease eternity in hell for you, what would you be prepared to do?

This is what I asked myself when considering the hierarchy of hell. Who will torment whom? How will the souls be corrupted to cause God to condemn them?

"For our struggle is not against flesh and blood, but against the rulers, against the authorities, against the powers of this world's darkness, and against the spiritual forces of evil in the heavenly realms" (Ephesians 6:12, BSB).

It is not other people who are the problem. We certainly see the person causing the problem. What we do not see is what drives them to evil conduct. That driving force is the army of darkness. This army is populated by soldiers as old as humanity. They have enmity toward humanity. They cannot be bargained with because their fate is already sealed.

They, however, are masters at offering humans a deal that we cannot refuse. It is the human exercise of free will that is leveraged against us. We have a choice knowing what is right and wrong; we can choose to do wrong if we want to. There is no lightning bolt from heaven for those who deliberately do wrong. The only reward for doing it right is, you get the opportunity to do it right again tomorrow. You will still face all the same temptations, but you have the power to choose; it is your God-given free will.

The enemy knows we have free will. In fact, the most potent law is God will not allow our free will to be infringed. The devil cannot make us sin. Many blame the devil for their bad behavior, saying, "The devil made me do it." But the truth is, the devil only tempted them. The person tempted has not sinned. Not yet. While being tempted, they are in a deliberation process.

I have "x" temptation. I deliberate. I know right from wrong. I know I should do what is right, but I think the wrong is so tempting. I have to make up my mind. If I do right, it is because I exercised my free will to do right. If I do wrong, it is because I exercised my free will to do wrong. No one made me do right or wrong; I chose what I did.

In that setup, the presentation of temptation, the army of darkness, has deployed its forces. There are many fallen angels working on it. Remember, these are soldiers in a declared war with millennia of combat experience against humankind. They have enmity for us and are very good at what they do.

Here is an example of how the army of darkness sets up an ambush. First, our focus is taken away from God. We have been distracted from God by something going on around us. This is the first step off the path of light.

As soon as we get distracted, something else grabs our attention. For this example, I will use being in a hurry to make an appointment. You realize you are running late and have to hurry. Now is when the minions of hell encroach upon us. Whatever we are doing, it takes longer than we want it to. Now we are climbing the ladder from functioning normally to rushing, to being faced with time constraint limitations that lead to stress and then anxiety.

If we continue to take steps further into the darkness, we will lose our reference to the lighted path. Now, this is my pet peeve. I call it out many times a day. If I am doing something, and it is not going in the most efficient manner possible, I will use profanity.

I have done it hundreds of times. As soon as I used foul language, whatever I was doing that was fighting me suddenly started working just fine. Why? Because the army of darkness has accomplished its mission. They have pushed me to the point I felt justified in using foul language. I imagine they are rolling on the floor laughing at me because they tempted me long enough to provoke my sin.

What I should do every time I feel my stress building is call upon the name of Jesus Christ. I could say something like, "Jesus, I don't know which little twerp demons are tempting me right now, but You do. Can You please make them go away? Thank You, Jesus."

This calling on the most powerful name under heaven is the key to victory over temptation. It is overcoming evil with good. This is what we are called to do. It is winning the spiritual war.

The better we can do this, the higher our save percentage. For those ones that get past us, and we do sin, we must ask for forgiveness. By the grace of God, we can be forgiven for the ones that get past us. As a result, we attain a perfect save percentage, and we are saved. I imagine that really irritates the army of darkness. They work so hard to trip us up, and even when we fall, God lifts us back up.

Any soldier worth his salt knows his enemy. As discussed above, the army of darkness certainly knows humankind. What do we know about the forces aligned against us? By now, we should be able to recognize light/good from dark/evil.

While we are in the light, doing good, we can see and navigate safely. Nobody can move us out of the light if we are determined to stay in it.

*No, in all these things we are more than conquerors through Him who loved us. For I am convinced that neither death nor life, neither angels nor principalities, neither the present nor the future, nor any powers, neither height nor depth, nor anything else in all creation, will be able to separate us from the love of God that is in Christ Jesus our Lord.*

Romans 8:37–39 (BSB)

When we exercise our free will to step wrong into darkness, then all the soldiers in the army of darkness are taking aim at us. They use every trick that humans have ever fallen for. It is a very long list.

"Sexual immorality, impurity, sensuality, idolatry, sorcery, enmity, strife, jealousy, fits of anger, rivalries, dissensions, divisions, envy, drunkenness, orgies, and things like these"
(Galatians 5:19–21, ESV).

It is important to remember that these attacks, the presentation of such temptations, worked on humans in the time of Noah, the time of Jesus, and still work today. These are not new. They are deployed against us because they have a proven track record (Ecclesiastes 1:9).

Normally such attacks come after we get distracted. Other times we begin to doubt the absolute supremacy of God, and from our doubt, temptations slither in. Another way we open the door to shadows is by fearing something other than God the most. Provoking the wrath of God on ourselves should be the greatest fear any person knows. You wouldn't try to steal from God, would you? What is the difference if you exercise your free will to deliberately do wrong?

That is when God must allow the natural consequences of our actions to cause us harm.

We still have the option to recognize our mistakes, repent, and ask God to forgive us. We can be forgiven. We should not make a habit of repeating the same mistakes. If one is truly sorry for what they have done wrong, they will change their behavior. That is something we struggle with throughout our lives. The enemy is ever present and will use anything against us. He has nothing to lose.

Now I will address those people who believe in the power of darkness to give them advantages in our fallen world. I base this interpretation on a county jail experience while I was waiting to go to prison and another experience I had in prison many years ago before I committed to the Lord and scripture in 1994.

Before I knew anything about discipleship to the written Word of God, I read the Bible for my own edification. I spent many hours each day reading the Bible like it was a regular book from any shelf in any library. It was all I had to do while I was waiting to go to court and learn the final disposition of my charges.

I was praying and meditating on my bunk in a four-man cell. I began to have a vivid dream. In the dream, I was following a person. I knew this person in real life. I was trying to get their attention to speak to them. They were focused on what they were doing and where they were going. In the dream, I had to hurry just to keep up with them. It seemed that every time I got to a corner, I looked around it just in time to see them make the next turn ahead of me.

The course we were taking was getting more and more difficult to traverse. I remember a particularly rickety-looking bridge between buildings about fifty stories up! In the dream, I had to pump myself up to even cross it. It was deteriorated and crumbling. The far side was one story higher than the side I started on. It had obviously broken and fell to wedge itself at this angle. There was only a small portion of it that was even crossable. It was a long way down!

After that was a steep stair, and it led to a secure door. Like a fire door. All metal, except for a small window high in the center. Looking through that window, I saw the person I was trying to catch speaking to a person behind a desk. The door wouldn't open for me. In a fit of rage, I tugged on the door until I broke it open. I saw the door behind the security desk close as I went in.

I went to the security desk. The person sitting behind the desk refused to let me by. I needed to get past this security point.

In frustration, I wound up and punched the security guard in the mouth. I was screaming, "Let me pass!"

The hit did little to the security guard. He got up and attempted to restrain me. We began to fight. I used everything I knew, from street fighting around my hometown to what the Marines taught me in close combat training and even some martial arts I had picked up from my Marine buddies. This security guard in my dream was too tough for me.

I remember him getting me in a bear hug and squeezing me. I couldn't breathe. I knew I was about to be suffocated. I refused to give up. I called on the name of Jesus Christ. That is when everything changed.

This security guard, whom I could not damage or injure, suddenly became frightened of me. I saw myself taking a deep breath. I inhaled deeply. The security guard was sucked into my lungs with my breath.

It was then that I woke out of my dream. When I looked around, the other three guys in the cell with me were all as far away as they could get. They were all staring at me. They were wide-eyed, and their mouths were hanging open. It took a few seconds, but one of them finally asked me, "Are you all right?"

When I told him, "I had a bad dream." They all looked at each other with disbelief.

The one who asked me if I was all right then said, "It looked like you were fighting for your life."

I was, but no one else saw who or what I was fighting. I cannot imagine what it looked like from their point of view. All I can tell you is these were grown men from the criminal element of society who were not afraid of police with guns. They looked terrified from what I had experienced in that dream.

I don't know what test that was or if I passed, all I can tell you is it impressed those other guys immensely. I was labeled *Sleeping Rambo* by them. Other prisoners were calling me sir and asking if I needed anything. It was a very weird experience for me.

This next event occurred after *catching the chain* and making it through reception center to a regular unit.

I was finally moved from reception to a regular unit. I was still unpacking, trying to figure out where to put my stuff. I was in a two-man cell. The other prisoner was not there. He was doing his prison job. I had the top bunk and a little space to put my belongings. The other resident was very neat and clean; all his stuff was organized and well cared for.

Another prisoner came to the bars in front of my cell. He was a white guy, bald-headed. He had prison tattoos covering his whole body. I noticed the "SS" lightning bolts on his face. On his throat was a Nazi warbird. This guy was somebody in prison. That was obvious.

I was the newest white guy in the cell block. I presumed this guy was a shot caller or sent by one to test me and see what I was about. He asked a few quick questions, where I was from, what I was in for, how long I was doing, then he stood up tall, leaned toward the bars, and said through clenched teeth, "Give me those colored pencils." He had a very hard glint in his eyes.

I stepped back from the bars; I kept eye contact with the dude until I was out of reach. I looked around the cell and saw the set of colored pencils that were my celly's. I smiled. I looked the dude in the eye, "I don't know who you are, but those colored pencils are not mine to give away. You could be my celly testing me to see what I am about."

The dude nodded as if to say, "*All right, you got me there,*" but he then said, "I will see you on the yard." And he walked off.

It was a few hours before my celly returned from work. He was an older white guy. I figured him for a banker type, probably an embezzler. I greeted him and went through the introductions common to convicts in prison. Then I told him the story of the tattoo guy. My celly laughed; he said, "Oh, that is just, so and so. He is just testing you. You did good. I am glad you are a standup guy. You never know what you are going to get around here."

That night, I was on my top bunk. My celly was on his bottom bunk, snoring. I was tossing and turning; I couldn't get the thoughts of tattoo guy and his implied threat out of my head. It was well after lights out. There are concrete floors, walls, and ceilings. Only the front of the cell has bars. The door is an automatic door controlled by the guards. They can key it open, but usually, they operate it from the board.

I felt another body get in my bunk with me! I reached out to fight whoever it was, assuming it was my celly. When I touched this body, I felt electric shock! It was the same as holding a live wire. I struggled with whatever this was until I felt myself about to black out. I called on the name of Jesus Christ. The body suddenly moved away from me.

I looked. It was night, and all lights were out, except for the exit signs at the end of each tier. The natural darkness was deep. I saw a supernatural darkness in the form of a humanoid levitating next to my top bunk. It slowly moved up and away. It went through the concrete wall. I remember seeing the unnatural darkness through the natural darkness. It was a very separate entity.

The next day on the prison yard, nobody came near me. No one spoke to me. It was as if I was not even visible. That was a spooky kind of feeling that reminded me of being homeless before I got in trouble.

Later at chow, I heard other convicts talking about another guy who had an accident in his cell. Somehow, he had a candle, the candle set something on fire, and the guy was burned. I don't know how bad. I never saw any smoke or fire; I didn't hear any alarms or see any emergency responders.

Later it was revealed that the guy who was burned was a devil worshipper!

That brought back the encounter with the body that night. I have always wondered what really happened. Was it an evil spirit sent to get me? Was it my calling on the name of Jesus Christ that defeated the evil spirit? Was the defeated evil spirit angry with the devil worshipper that summoned it? Those things roll around in my overactive imagination every time I think about those events.

All I can say for sure is that I know what I experienced. Those other convicts talking at chow time had no idea who I was or what I had experienced. There was a certain cold, dark, consuming emptiness that hung in the air like a bad smell. Whatever it was, it made me a believer in dark/evil spirits.

It is not very likely today that a parent would burn their child in a fire as a sacrifice to the devil. It might be happening; I don't know. As evil as that is, it is mentioned in scripture. Certain people who believe in the power of darkness will make sacrifices to the devil in exchange for some perceived benefit. It is expressly outlawed in scripture.

Other things on that forbidden list include divination, fortune telling, interpretations, sorcery, charms, mediums, necromancy, and one who inquires of the dead. Witchcraft, familiar spirits, astrology, tarot, numerology, Ouija board, and basically anything that displaces God as our source of comfort and confidence (Deuteronomy 18:10–11, Leviticus 20:27, Leviticus 19:26, Exodus 22:18).

When we pray, we must consider the army of darkness, the temptations they use to trick us, and the people who partake of darkness. Unless we pray to God for His information, knowledge, wisdom, understanding, discernment, deliberative capacity, sagacity, enlightenment, sapience, and reasoning, we are denying God His rightful place as the all-knowing.

Most often, God knows what we need before we ask for it. If we tell him, "God, You know what I need, let Your will be done," we give power to God to work in our behalf (Matthew 6:8).

In this crazy mixed-up world, it can be very confusing to live rightly according to scripture. Maintaining focus on God. Putting God first. Reading scripture every day. Praying continuously. Practicing what we understand the scriptures say. All these things together give us strength against the evil one and his army of darkness. They are for real, and they are coming hard for believers at the request of anti-Christians. Some anti-Christians have delved into depravity to such an extent that they sold their souls to the devil for some influence to receive infernal favor.

If we are not taught to anticipate such possibilities, being caught off guard by them can be life-shattering. If we do not know what to expect or how to deal with it, our bad reaction can lead to panic and personal harm. Keeping our wits, trusting God, and never giving in to fear, doubt, distraction, or selfish pursuits is winning the spiritual battle.

God bless you can be the best soldier of light you possibly can be.

# Chapter 16

## THE FATAL FLAW IN COMMERCIAL FAITH

I understand people who have never heard the Gospel before are up against a lot when they first decide to come to Christ. I get it; faith teachers want to reach as many people as possible. Walking in faith certainly can be intimidating for someone just starting out. I do believe the greatest gift one person can give another is a more accurate understanding of scripture and God.

It is not my intent to point out flaws in anyone else working in the ministry of faith. I only want to point out the three levels of faith as I see them. A person new to faith is said to be an infant in faith. They need the milk of scripture to get started. Like an infant growing, it takes a while on the milk for them to develop to the point where they can take solid food. That is called the mature person of faith who can take the meat of scripture. I would like to take it one step further and say the disciple of Scripture is ready for the mana of the word.

What I want to address here is the difference between each level of faith. A person who needs the milk will be discouraged or confused by the meat and/or mana of the word. There are too many people, places, and events in scripture to keep straight when just starting out.

After a person has read the entire Bible cover to cover one time, receiving the milk of the word, they are only able to retain and actively use a small percentage of the whole book. That is natural. No one can absorb that much material in one read-through and be an expert on all it contains.

That is why I like to say a person's walk in faith is a lifelong pursuit. The journey is not complete because the believer finished reading the

Bible one time. I encourage every person of faith to immediately start over reading it again. Build off the daily reading habit. I promise, the second time through, each believer will gain more scriptural insight to add to what they gained in the first reading. I guarantee it. This continuous rereading will strengthen the understanding one has. It will increase that percentage of scripture retained, and the believer will be able to put even more of it into active use daily.

After the second or third time through, the believer will start to recognize what they received from the previous readings, and now it reveals a different aspect of itself. No other book is like this. It will be evidence to the believer that something wonderful is going on between them and their Creator. The same print on the same page teaches me something different when I read it more than once. That is miraculous!

I suggest that this is the point in a walk of faith that the believer is transitioning from the milk stage to the meat stage. Going into the fourth and fifth reading, the believer is now cognizant of the historical period, the people, places, and events in scripture are familiar. At least they can recognize them when they read about them. This is when the believer gets more curious about everything scriptural. They begin to read different translations, check definitions in the concordance, and maybe pick up a Bible commentary on their favorite book of the Bible.

This is also the point at which the believer can go from being in a faith-based group as a student to becoming a leader of such a group, doing the teaching. God puts different things on different people's hearts. We call these the *gifts of the spirit*. As we grow in our understanding and mature in our active knowledge of and practical application of scripture in our daily lives, God working through us happens. As we allow ourselves to be the conduit through which God works in the world, we become active participants in "God's will be done on earth as it is in heaven." That is from the Lord's Prayer, if you recognize it.

It has been my experience that many people on fire for the Lord get to this point and don't know there is another step they can take. Then after so much time, they burn out. It is true if you are not growing, you are dying. It is the same with faith. If you are not growing your faith, your faith is dying.

How do we grow beyond the mature faith and the meat of scripture?

I believe that each scripture presents three interpretations. This coincides with the Trinity of Father, Son, and Holy Spirit. Scripture is divinely inspired, that is, from God, who is all three. His words apply to all three aspects of God. Like God the Father, scripture has a spiritual aspect/interpretation. The same as the Son, which is God in the living flesh, each scripture has a physical aspect/interpretation. This also applies to the Holy Spirit as the doer of God's will; each scripture has an aspect/interpretation that varies with the person reading it and what stage of their life they are in and what they are going through at the time they read it.

I call this the mana of scripture. The Holy Spirit opening the scriptures to mature believers in ways they have not previously considered or experienced. Going from meat to mana is as big a step as going from milk to meat.

Instead of only considering how each scripture applies to self in the moment it is read, the believer taking the mana of scripture considers how it would apply to children, adults, senior citizens, the prince, the priest, the prophet, as well as the poor, the laborer, and the artist. As many perspectives as one can imagine, each scripture can be considered.

It is this diversity of the deliberative capacity in due diligence that grows a mature believer into a disciple. It doesn't matter who seeks scriptural answers from a disciple of Scripture; the scripture provides the answer. It is the disciple's vast active knowledge of scripture and long history of applying it in everyday life that makes it possible to find the answer in scripture.

Now that I have clarified the three levels of scriptural competency as I see it, I want to say that the best leaders in faith meet their students where their students are. A good teacher learns what their student needs before they begin teaching.

God has placed the desire in my heart to share the greatest gift I have ever received. I do enjoy many television evangelists. I like to see people on fire for the Lord, teaching with zeal and enthusiasm. I am not a great orator. I write much better than I can speak.

I do admire all those great speakers with every inspiring message they produce. God is working through them! At the same time, I have noticed, that is, God has shown me, something we can do together to make it better for all believers who desire to be students and eventually disciples of Scripture.

I see this theme in commercial faith media: faith leaders saying that just the belief in Jesus Christ saves people. This is good scripture, it is a valid teaching, but there is more. Jesus told us:

> *Don't misunderstand why I have come. I did not come to abolish the law of Moses or the writings of the prophets. No, I came to accomplish their purpose. I tell you the truth, until heaven and earth disappear, not even the smallest detail of God's law will disappear until its purpose is achieved.*

> Matthew 5:17–18 (NLT)

Jesus said, "The law of Moses" and one step farther, the "writings of the prophets." It is more than just obedience to the law; it is also applying the lessons taught by the prophets that we must obey.

Jesus told us, "Not even the smallest detail of God's law will disappear until its purpose is achieved."

I take that to mean not until all the saved are in heaven and all the condemned are in hell will the law stop being important. The timing of this is of great importance. The "*Law*" (that which convicts) is in full force and effect until those who pass have passed, and those who fail have failed. The reason that is important is because all those saved have exercised their free will to conduct their physical lives in accordance with the laws in scripture. They have walked the walk in the light.

On the flip side of that coin, those who are condemned have exercised their free will to conduct their physical lives contrary to the laws in scripture. They have stumbled off the illuminated walkway and fallen into darkness.

If a believer is never told that this is the consequence of disobedience, they will feel cheated when they find themselves in an eternal bath of hellfire and brimstone. The sulfur bubbles really stink!

I feel it is my duty and obligation to express this more accurate understanding of scripture to all who would believe. No, faith is not easy. It is not just one hour spent once a week in a church. Faith is a lifelong pursuit. Like a hobby, sport, or career. We put effort into such things every day. We are educated on the subject. We apply what we learn to produce better output.

Eventually, with time, practice, and diligence, we become experts or professionals in that area.

Why do we not view our faith in a similar light?

Often when people have to make a choice between a worldly function and a faith function, we will sacrifice the faith function. The excuse is we do not have the time to spend on our faith, it does not pay the bills, or it is not the way we enjoy spending our free time.

If those excuses seem to be a fair trade for our eternal soul, let's look at the value God puts on the individual human soul.

"And what do you benefit if you gain the whole world but lose your own soul? Is anything worth more than your soul?" (Mark 8:36–37, NLT).

Do we think that the Creator of the heavens and the earth does not know the dollar value of the planet we live on? He made it, us, and the dollar. He knows the value of each. Let's also consider if we lost our soul, what can we give to have it returned to us?

"If anyone is ashamed of me and my message in these adulterous and sinful days, the Son of Man will be ashamed of that person when he returns in the glory of his Father with the holy angels" (Mark 8:38, NLT).

That means there is nothing a person can give to get their soul back once it is lost. For all those people who think it is funny, prosperous, or worth saying, "I would sell my soul for a cup of coffee," you are under a powerful delusion.

> *and with every wicked deception directed against those who are perishing, because they refused the love of the truth that would have saved them. For this reason God will send them a powerful delusion so that they believe the lie, in order that judgment may come upon all who have disbelieved the truth and delighted in wickedness.*
>
> 2 Thessalonians 2:10–12 (BSB)

Some people will say they don't believe in that part of the Bible. Other people will argue that the new covenant excludes people from following the law. It does not matter what a person believes; what is written in scripture is what will happen. As far as the new covenant, Jesus is the one who said He came to fulfill the law and prophets.

As shown above, the individual human soul is worth more to God than the dollar value of planet earth. The cliché "the world is not enough" is fitting. Each person should consider that scriptural truth when deliberating on the weight to give spending time in faith. How important it becomes to ask for forgiveness for all our sins each day.

"The soul who sins is the one who will die. A son will not bear the iniquity of his father, and a father will not bear the iniquity of his son. The righteousness of the righteous man will fall upon him, and the wickedness of the wicked man will fall upon him" (Ezekiel 18:20, BSB).

It is nice that God is a God of love and will forgive us.

> *But if the wicked man turns from all the sins he has committed, keeps all My statutes, and does what is just and right, he will surely live; he will not die. None of the transgressions he has committed will be held against him. Because of the righteousness he has practiced, he will live.*
>
> Ezekiel 18:21–22 (BSB)

This is a great expectation for us. To obtain this hope, we must ask for forgiveness every day.

"If we confess our sins, he is faithful and just and will forgive us our sins and purify us from all unrighteousness" (1 John 1:9, NIV).

*Jesus replied, "If anyone loves Me, he will keep My word. My Father will love him, and We will come to him and make Our home with him. Whoever does not love Me does not keep My words. The word that you hear is not My own, but it is from the Father who sent Me. All this I have spoken to you while I am still with you."*

John 14:23–25 (BSB)

"If you love me, you will keep my commandments" (John 14:15, ESV).

"By this we know that we love the children of God: when we love God and keep His commandments" (1 John 5:2, BSB).

If we profess to know Jesus Christ and claim eternal salvation through Christ by our knowledge of Him, it makes sense that we also must be obedient to the laws and prophets as they are fulfilled in the first coming of Christ, and Jesus told us Himself we must do so to inherit eternal life.

For any person buying off on the commercial faith sentiment that just believing in the person of Jesus Christ is enough to gain eternal salvation, I say pray about it in light of the scriptures presented above.

The commercial line on faith is:

"For all have sinned, and fall short of the glory of God" (Romans 3:23, BSB).

"But God proves His love for us in this: While we were still sinners, Christ died for us" (Romans 5:8, BSB).

"For the wages of sin is death; but the gift of God is eternal life through Jesus Christ our Lord" (Romans 6:23, BSB).

"that if you confess with your mouth Jesus as Lord, and believe in your heart that God raised Him from the dead, you will be saved" (Romans 10:9, BSB).

For "Everyone who calls on the name of the Lord will be saved" (Romans 10:13, BSB).

This is good scripture, and it is to be believed. The problem I have with it as the only requirement for salvation is that it is too easy, excludes the words of Jesus Christ, and opens people up to fatal faith for their souls.

If a person goes by, "I know Jesus, I am good," they may forget to ask for forgiveness of the sins they commit. If we do not obtain the remission of guilt for our sins, God will not hear our prayers.

"Whoever turns his ear away from hearing the law, even his prayer is detestable" (Proverbs 28:9, BSB).

"We know that God does not listen to sinners, but He does listen to the one who worships Him and does His will" (John 9:31, BSB).

"And do not bring sorrow to God's Holy Spirit by the way you live. Remember, he has identified you as his own, guaranteeing that you will be saved on the day of redemption" (Ephesians 4:30, NLT).

"So I spoke to you, but you would not listen. You rebelled against the command of the LORD and presumptuously went up into the hill country" (Deuteronomy 1:43, BSB).

First, we are told by God what He expects of us. Then we disobey.

"Then the Amorites who lived in the hills came out against you and chased you like a swarm of bees. They routed you from Seir all the way to Hormah" (Deuteronomy 1:44, BSB).

In our disobedience, we suffer God's punishment.

"And you returned and wept before the LORD, but He would not listen to your voice or give ear to you" (Deuteronomy 1:45, BSB).

Until we confess our sins to God, ask Him for His forgiveness, and He grants it, we are not going to be heard when we pray to Him.

*On that day My anger will burn against them, and I will abandon them and hide My face from them, so that they will be consumed, and many troubles and afflictions will befall them. On that day they will say, "Have not these disasters come upon us because our God is no longer with us?"*

Deuteronomy 31:17 (BSB)

Scripture tells us why the Lord is displeased with us, the reason He will not listen to our prayers.

*You ignored the Rock who brought you forth; you forgot the God who gave you birth. When the LORD saw this, He rejected them, provoked to anger by His sons and daughters. He said: "I will hide My face from them; I will see what will be their end. For they are a perverse generation—children of unfaithfulness."*

Deuteronomy 32:18–20 (BSB)

After reading all the previous scriptures about God refusing to hear the prayers of the disobedient, it makes sense why so many bad things are happening in our world today. We, as a civilization, have bought into the false belief that all we need to do to be saved is confess that Jesus Christ is our Lord and Savior.

That is a milk-level faith. It is true that people who believe in Jesus Christ as the only-begotten Son of God have access to redemption for their sins. A more accurate understanding at the meat level of faith is we have to ask Jesus to forgive us of our sins every day. We do not want to forget one day and be in sin the following day, which means God will not hear our prayers when we pray to Him.

The longer we go without being forgiven for our sins, the longer God does not hear us. I believe every time we pray, we should begin our prayer with asking God to forgive us for all our sins. That ensures us that God will hear what we are praying for.

I think this is a good place to start teaching new believers the milk of scripture. The milk is the most essential core value of scripture. There is more to the story, however. After the milk is the meat of scripture, a deeper understanding accompanied by greater application of it in our daily lives. I would take it one step farther, to the mana of scripture. An exhaustive understanding of all scripture accompanied by a comprehensive application of it in our daily lives.

The good Lord has put this on my heart for some time. The longer I do nothing, the more intense the feeling I have. Many faith leaders may be speaking to the new believer with the milk of scripture. Over time new believers grow and need the meat of scripture to continue to blossom. Further on, the mature believer is called to discipleship, making new believers. This is when the mana of scripture is needed. I have two thoughts intertwined on the issue.

First, it is less than ideal for a faith leader to tell people pursuing their faith that all they need to do is believe in the person of Jesus Christ to get a full boat ride to paradise for eternity with God. Believing our Savior lived and walked this earth is the first step toward eternal salvation.

If that is all that a believer is taught, when it comes time to face God in judgment, Jesus will tell that person, "Not everyone who says to Me, 'Lord, Lord,' will enter the kingdom of heaven, but only he who does the will of My Father in heaven" (Matthew 7:21, BSB).

The key phrase is: "[...] only he who does the will of My Father in heaven." The will of the Father in heaven is that we conduct ourselves in obedience to the commandments, laws, statutes, and ordinances of scripture.

The second thought is the enemy, Lucifer, the rebellious, defeated, cast out, condemned, and cursed, is an extremely lethal opponent. He wants to deceive as many people as possible. Why? So, we can suffer the same fate he is waiting for himself. He knows his punishment is real. The devil is good at what he does. The unfortunate truth is he will deceive the whole world. What that means is people with free will can be tricked into believing a lie. Free will does not make a person perfect.

> *In everything, then, do to others as you would have them do to you. For this is the essence of the Law and the Prophets. Enter through the narrow gate. For wide is the gate and broad is the way that leads to destruction, and many enter through it. But small is the gate and narrow the way that leads to life, and only a few find it.*

Matthew 7:12–14 (BSB)

If you notice, it says, "[...] this is the essence of the Law and the Prophets." These are the things that Jesus told us He came to fulfill. Belief that Jesus Christ was a real person who walked this earth, was crucified, died, and resurrected on the third day is key to salvation. It is not all there is to it, however. We must also be obedient to the law and apply the teachings of the prophets.

> *Even if we accept human testimony, the testimony of God is greater. For this is the testimony that God has given about His Son. Whoever believes in the Son of God has this testimony within him; whoever does not believe God has made Him out to be a liar, because he has not believed in the testimony that God has given about His Son.*

1 John 5:9–10 (BSB)

Jesus Christ died under the law, a willing sacrifice and ransom from the law of sin and death to reconcile us back to God. If we throw out the law and prophets' part of this equation, the sacrifice loses its ransom power, and we cannot be reconciled back to God. That would be pointless.

Therefore, we need to be obedient to the law and prophets as much as we believe in the person of Jesus Christ to attain salvation. "As the body without the spirit is dead, so faith without deeds is dead" (James 2:26, BSB).

We have established there is more to faith than just a belief in Jesus Christ. What more do we need to do to give ourselves the best chance to attain eternal salvation?

Remember what the Holy Bible stands for.

Holy Bible equals "He Only Left You Basic Instructions Before Leaving Earth."

I feel it is worth mentioning that these basic instructions grow with a person as they study scripture and apply them in their daily life.

What does it mean to be obedient?

Obey

the Bible

Especially

During

Intense

Emotionally

Negative

Circumstances

Every chance you get

How do we become mature in our walk of faith? Maturity is thinking about what your words and deeds will accomplish before you speak the words or do the acts.

Why is being impulsive so bad? Impulsivity is saying or doing whatever comes to mind without the filter of maturity.

Why are we judged for the words we speak? When we speak a thought, our words give energy to the thought. Both the enemy of God and God Himself hear the words. We have to be forgiven for God to hear our prayers. The devil, however, accuses us before God every chance he gets. Our words will be used against us if possible. We must very carefully mark the words we speak. Two common failings are words spoken in anger and words spoken in jest. Controlling one's own speech is often the hardest task to accomplish.

Why are we judged for the things we do? The things we do reflect on the one we claim to be our God. If we claim to be Christians and do something sinful, we should immediately repent. If we let our sins go, they start to pile up on us. Sin is cumulative. One little sin is enough to convict us of violating the whole of the law. If we pray while unrepentant, God will not hear our prayers; we get further in debt to sin. We carry huge burdens of sin. We cannot understand why we are suffering. We read the Bible, go to church, pray, ask God for His will to be done in our lives, and we ask in Jesus' mighty name, but nothing good is coming to us.

The solution is to ask God to forgive us for all our sins. Every outstanding sin needs forgiving. Every sin, iniquity, transgression, and backsliding. All those we know about and the ones we don't know about. How do we not know we committed a sin that we need to be forgiven for? If we don't know what the six-hundred-plus laws are, it is a safe bet one of us miss stepped and does not realize it. In this case, it really is better to be safe than sorry.

# Chapter 17

## A More Powerful Way to Pray

With the foregoing as a table setting for a more accurate understanding of scripture as a disciple of Scripture, what we were meant to be, what we are up against, and how to detect threats, let us now move into how we pray more effectively. The first and most fundamental thing to believe and put faith in is that *God*, Jesus Christ, and the Holy Spirit do fight for us. The second most fundamental thing to believe and put your faith in is that Lucifer, Satan, the devil, and all the rebellious angels, are defeated, cursed, and cast out. They are doomed to failure in their fight against *God*.

"[...] with great fury the devil has come down to you, knowing he has only a short time"

(Revelation 12:12, BSB).

First is to never doubt the absolute supremacy of Father *God Yahweh* in all things, all places, and at all times simultaneously. This is your confidence in *God's* capability.

Second is to never fear anything more than provoking the wrath of *God* on yourself. Even a miserable death as a faithful disciple of Scripture is more beneficial than any other kind. This is you being *God*-fearing, which is the beginning of spiritual understanding.

Third is to be seeking *God's* will in your life. If you do it your way, *God* is much less inclined to hear your prayers. (Like praying to win the lottery, even if you intend to give your tithe out of the winnings.) We are not trying to win the game of life here on earth; we are playing for eternity and trying to store up our treasures in heaven.

With those ground rules for more effective prayer, some fine tuning is still needed.

*The Seven Laws of Prayer*

1. Have a pure heart,

2. forgive others who have made you suffer,

3. have good and just motives,

4. have a very strong and stubborn faith,

5. have the will of *God* be your prayer,

6. pray in the name of Jesus Christ,

7. pray in the Holy Spirit.[2]

After I found these "Seven Laws of Prayer" on the internet, I thoughtfully considered them and became convinced that we could add to them. I came up with Laws of Prayer 8 to 21.

8. Pray with thanksgiving,

9. pray as Jesus Christ prayed for us,

10. as Jesus Christ has gone to prepare a place for us;

11. by the power of the resurrection of Jesus Christ,

---

2      Retrieved from Christian Assemblies International (CAI), P. O. Box 888, Coffs Harbour, NSW 2450 Australia on July 15, 2018

12. by the power of the ascension of Jesus Christ,

13. by the power of Jesus Christs' promised return in victory.

14. *God*, I cannot do this, but I know you can.

15. I believe in Jesus Christ being the only-begotten Son of *God* that He is my Lord and Savior; as He is an heir to eternal life, those faithful to Him also become children of God and thereby co-heirs to eternal life so we can be reconciled back to *God* as *He* had originally intended before the fall from grace in the Garden of Eden (our first estate).

16. (For spouses.) We are one flesh blessed by You, *God*, in holy matrimony; what ails one ails both of us, one's joy is the joy of both of us; You know what we need, Father *God*. Bless us with all the blessings that *You* can bestow upon us.

17. I pray for all those who believe in Jesus Christ as their Lord and Savior that *God* bless them all with all the blessings that *God* can bestow upon them.

18. I pray for all those who do not believe in Jesus Christ as their Lord and Savior that they may come to know Jesus Christ as their Lord and Savior.

19. Father, forgive me for all my sins, iniquities, transgressions, and backslidings. Wash me with the blood of Jesus Christ, fill me with the Holy Spirit that I may be found without blemish, blameless in Your sight. Lord, hear my prayer in Jesus' mighty name.

20. My almighty, all-knowing, in every place at all times, Father God, provide me with all the information, knowledge, understanding, wisdom, deliberative capacity, discernment, and sagacity required to maintain a right relationship with You to overcome the evil of the anti-Christians with the good You intend for us, Father God.

21. (Bedtime prayer.) Thank You, Father God! We won another day. Now I lay me down to sleep. Send Your guardian angels to watch over me while I sleep. Set a hedge of protection around me, my family, my house, my things, and my stuff. Give me inspirational dreams. Show me what I need to know to fulfill my part in Your plan for me so that I understand it. In Jesus' mighty name.

The reason praying in such a way is powerful is because we are quoting Bible scripture in our prayers. These are *God's* words. Much as we feel obligated to fulfill our words when they are used back on us, *God* will not let His words return empty (Isiah 55:11).

Some of those worldly people who seek to rid the world of Christianity use occult means (Deuteronomy 18:10–12); they employ mediums, spiritists, numerology, and astrology; they use witchcraft, divination, demonology, and devil worship. They conduct sacrifices, rites, and rituals meant to unleash harmful spirits against our faith. Scripture forbids the use of such things and admits such things have real power, but greater is he who is in you than he who is in the world. (1 John 4:4). A good prayer warrior understands these things and prays for God's protection and His warring angels to intercede on our behalf.

An important issue is that of anti-Christian's sacrificing to other gods. The way I understand it: when a sacrifice is made for evil purposes, the more innocent the victim, the greater the reward. Additionally, the more pain and suffering inflicted on the victim, the higher the reward. As sickening as this is, it is what happens.

I am not denying anybody else their right to practice their religion however they see fit. I am simply pointing out that a person can use their free will to do whatever they want. It may be skirting the law, but God sees all. Those who think they are unobserved by anyone who would complain are mistaken.

That is why I like heartbeat laws for *unborn people*. If lack of a heartbeat is evidence of death, then the presence of a heartbeat necessarily must be evidence of life. I believe that the overturning of Roe v. Wade by the Supreme Court has ruffled some anti-Christian feathers.

It has prompted executive orders to reinstate abortion as a right, and legislators have hurried through legislation to make it like it was. Is that not repugnant to justice? The Supreme Court just ruled against it, so they remake the same laws and put them back in place? It is a miscarriage of justice.

Why do such people insist on killing children in the womb?

It promotes promiscuity and relieves accountability. Now for the most sickening part: what happens to the "waste tissue" post abortion?

We know it is illegal to perform medical research/experimentation on living humans. It is not, however, illegal to do so on waste tissue. Many biological research entities buy the waste tissue from abortion clinics so they can skirt the law against human research. This practice is highly offensive to me!

One case study that I am aware of, the business admitted participating in such research but vehemently denied any fetal tissue was in its products. I say boycott their products and vote with your dollars.

Another thing that disgusts me is the cure for cancer donation scheme. For over fifty years, the standard medical response to any kind of cancer is chemotherapy and radiation. I have two statements about chemo; first, have you seen how much they charge for a single round of chemotherapy? At that price, who needs donations? Second, I am still waiting for anyone to explain to me how chemo distinguishes between cancer cells and healthy ones.

Now my thoughts on radiation treatment. Number one, radiation is the biggest reason we do not have a plethora of nuclear power plants supplying us with an abundance of electrical power at a low price. Secondly, when I was an infantryman in the United States Marine Corps, our government taught me that there is no such thing as good radiation. How does it become medicine if you have cancer?

One more thing that I cannot wrap my head around is all the advertisements for medicines that have more and worse side effects than what they are trying to treat. How can something that does more harm than good be considered marketable for medicine?

To me, it is snake oil. Which is fitting because the devil is often characterized as a serpent or snake. A dragon is just a really big snake! I understand people demand treatments for illness. I get it; the people who make medicine do so with the best of intentions. My question is, why not use natural remedies?

If there is something in nature that helps the situation, why not distill that down to a concentrated form and use that for medicine? Why do we have to use chemical concoctions that do more harm than good? It was suggested to me that no one can patent a natural substance, so there is no money in it. Then the light comes on. Vendors of medicine sell one pill for a specific problem, then the patient develops other symptoms, and more pills are prescribed to fix those. It becomes a self-sustaining train of medical issues. Who could be responsible for such a travesty? Follow the money.

I knew a woman who got fed up with this very circumstance in her life. In a fit of frustration, she swiped approximately fifteen separate pill bottles off her kitchen counter into the waste basket. At that time, she said, "If I am going to die, I am going to die healthy!"

She began to walk. Her first walk was from her front porch to the city sidewalk in front of her house. That was all she could manage before she was winded. After a few weeks, she was able to walk around her block. Within two months, she was walking four blocks to get an ice cream for a treat!

At her next doctor's appointment, her doctor was amazed at the progress she had made. He asked her, "What are you doing differently?"

She answered him, "I quit taking all the pills you prescribed me, and I started walking."

She exercised her free will with informed dissent to make her personal medical decision. I am not a doctor, and I do not recommend anyone do what she did, but you do have free will, and you can do your own research.

This woman lived another thirty years medicine free. When she did pass, it was not because of any illness she was prescribed medicine for that she dumped in the trash thirty years earlier.

These things and so many more are what I believe are the principalities and powers we struggle against. I see the abortion activists and the donate to cancer research people all believing in the cause they represent. They are using their free will to give an effort for what they believe is a good thing. My question is, are they aware of the negative aspects of what they are representing? Just as there is informed consent, I also believe in informed dissent.

If a person exercises due diligence and investigates the methods and processes of such institutions, the negative side effects become apparent. As stated above, everyone has the God-given right of free will. God will hold everyone accountable for their thoughts, words, and deeds. As a disciple of Scripture and understanding how God wants His children to treat each other (Luke 6:31), how is it a loving act to terminate a life in the womb or call it medicine to destroy healthy tissue? I imagine the good Lord has a special cup of wrath for those who promote such evil acts.

I imagine the wrath of God going out ahead of each prayer warrior, like when God drove the inhabitants out of the Promised Land ahead of the Israelites. When we face our enemies and the principalities and powers, and we are going through personal trials and tribulations in our walk of faith, I encourage you to fight like, "God has gone out before you" (Deuteronomy 31:8, BSB).

Imagine the wrath of God fighting ahead of you as you go into battle. What would that look like?

"But if in spite of all this you do not obey Me, but continue to walk in hostility toward Me, then I will walk in fury against you, and I, even I, will punish you sevenfold for your sins" (Leviticus 26:27–28, BSB).

> *I will make them a horror and an offense to all the kingdoms of the earth, a disgrace and an object of scorn, ridicule, and cursing wherever I have banished them. And I will send against them sword and famine and plague, until they have perished from the land that I gave to them and their fathers.*
>
> Jeremiah 24:9–10 (BSB)

"The wrath of God is being revealed from heaven against all the godlessness and wickedness of men who suppress the truth by their wickedness" (Romans 1:18, BSB).

God sees all and knows all. He knows what is in our hearts. He knows our every thought. He knows our motives and intentions. He allows us free will to do what we know is wrong. He does this because all things work together for the greater glory of God (Romans 8:28–29). It might help to explain the situation the way I see it in my mind. The following is a mix of resources found on the internet and other places listed in the "Bibliography" and my own vision of events.

Speaking of the evil one, *the enemy* of a more accurate understanding of scripture.

"How you have fallen from heaven, O day star, son of the dawn! You have been cut down to the ground, O destroyer of nations" (Isaiah 14:12, BSB).

"I saw Satan fall like lightning from heaven. The prophet and the Savior speak of Lucifer's fall from heaven" (Luke 10:18, BSB).

"[...] that ancient serpent called the devil and Satan, the deceiver of the whole world. He was hurled to the earth, and his angels with him" (Revelation 12:9, BSB).

How many angels came with him?

The dragon's "tail swept a third of the stars from the sky, tossing them to the earth" (Revelation 12:4, BSB).

"For if God did not spare the angels when they sinned, but cast them deep into hell, placing them in chains of darkness to be held for judgment" (2 Peter 2:4, BSB).

"And the angels who did not stay within their own domain, but abandoned their proper dwelling, these He has kept in eternal chains under darkness, bound for judgment on that great day" (Jude 1:6, BSB).

The fallen dragon, Lucifer, Satan, the devil, and all his followers cast down to earth from heaven would be understandably irritated by their predicament. No longer able to enter the kingdom of heaven to make war, they would very likely focus their efforts against *God*, on *His* creation.

The devil's thinking would be, "If I can't rule in heaven, then I will destroy *God's* creation on earth." Play the spoiler. I believe the creation of humankind is the catalyst for the war in heaven.

What is the enemy's motivation to afflict humankind?

I believe that Lucifer, then the most powerful angel in heaven, became jealous of *God's* favor showered on this new creation. I imagine this extremely powerful angelic being viewing the new creation with disdain. Lucifer asks *God* the question, "What is it made out of?"

*God* answers, "He is made from the dust of the earth."

Lucifer looks at the puny man and says, "It's a dirt ball?"

*God* tells Lucifer, "I formed man from the dust of the ground and breathed the breath of life into his nostrils, and the man became a living being" (Genesis 2:7, BSB).

Lucifer watches the new creation in the Garden of Eden. Lucifer sees the new creation as soft, weak, ignorant, and of little use for anything important.

Then *God* is walking in the Garden with Adam. Lucifer is wondering what *God* is thinking while *He* is slumming it with the dirt ball.

Lucifer begins to harbor ill will toward the creation. He speaks to his fellow angels. One-third of the angels in the host of heaven are sympathetic to Lucifer and his argument against *God's* preferential treatment of the newer creation.

I imagine Lucifer and the angels with him playing the seniority card. "We were here first! We deserve better than this new creation. We have been around a long time. We have proven ourselves over time. We cannot accept being leap-frogged by this 'dirt ball'!"

*God* would probably be amused by the petty and insignificant gesture of *His* previously created beings, the angels. "This creation is My labor of love. Yes, he is new and untried. That is why I have to be with him. To answer his questions. Show him how things work. Prepare him for his purpose in *My* plan."

Lucifer would have recognized that *God* was not going to be dissuaded from *His* preoccupation with the new creation. Lucifer might have considered that while *God* was so preoccupied, he might be able to pull off a coup in heaven. That is when Lucifer devised a plan to try and take over the rulership of heaven. He persuaded one-third of the angels in the host of heaven to join his coup attempt.

The Bible tells us he lost that fight. I imagine the fallen Lucifer bitter in his defeat but still unwilling to accept a back seat to the newer creation. Out of a sense of vindictiveness, he deiced to spoil the thing *God* prized, *His* creation.

Lucifer, now Satan and the devil, studied the creation in the Garden of Eden. He learned the one rule that *God* had established for the man and the woman. He devised a plan to manipulate the new creations into violating the only rule *God* gave them.

I imagine that playing spoiler was a disgrace for the fallen angel. He couldn't win a straight-up fight with *God*. Now he was in the form of a serpent, crawling upon his belly. He was sneaking into the garden. He was afraid of being seen by *God*. His plan was to trick the new creation into violating *God's* one rule. He planned to do it by questioning what the creation understood *God* meant by what *He* said.

The new creation was not experienced in dealing with deceit and manipulative semantics. The fallen angel knew this. The devil picked on Eve because Adam relayed *God's* rule to her. She didn't hear the rule for herself from *God's* mouth. The devil leveraged his strength against the woman's weakness.

I believe that the fallen Lucifer anticipated and expected *God* to immediately kill the newer creation for breaking the rule. When it turned out that *God* had a different solution to the "death clause" for Adam and Eve, the devil had to invent a different way to spoil the newer creation of *God*.

As humans began to populate the earth, the devil and his fellow betrayers and mutineers saw the daughters of men. They found human women attractive. They wanted to mate with them and did quite freely. The Bible tells us that the product of such unions is the Nephilim (Genesis 6:4).

This was occurring up to the time of the great Flood of Noah's time. The Flood was supposed to kill off all the Nephilim.

After the Flood, something changed. Human life expectancy was curtailed to one hundred and twenty years. I don't know how that would ensure a human female could no longer mate with a fallen angel. Unless that change in life expectancy also included a genetic block to the possibility of human conception with the fallen angels.

It results in the devil having to re-invent his human defiling strategies and tactics yet again. Throughout the rest of the Old Testament and into the New Testament, from the Flood to the immaculate conception, humans fail to be obedient to *God* over and over again. The devil is stealing souls at an ever-increasing rate.

*God* decides to change that trend by sending *His* only-begotten Son to earth. Imagine the devil seeing one of those responsible for his exile on earth coming into the world as a human infant. The helpless child was prophesied to be the savior of the planet. The devil knew if he killed that child, he would thwart *God's* plan.

*God* knew that as well. He wasn't about to let the devil get close to achieving his goals. The only way the devil would kill *God's* Son was the way *God* intended for it to happen.

After thousands of years of getting close to spoiling the creation just to have *God* change the rules again, the devil was desperate to take that child's life. He caused King Herod to order every male child under three years old born in Judea to be killed. That is plumb drastic!

Every time the devil's minions got close to capturing the Son of *God* as a child, an angel of the *Lord* would warn the Savior's family. They would make a hasty escape and further enrage the devil. This pattern continues up to the point when Jesus Christ begins His ministry on earth.

Now Jesus is a grown man and can handle what the devil throws at Him. It was not until the appointed time that *God* allowed Jesus Christ to be captured. Many biblical prophecies were fulfilled by these events. It was meant to happen this way.

The devil was so full of murderous blood lust that he failed to see the trap *God* set for him. The devil ran straight into the ambush. The devil was dancing for joy because he perceived victory when Jesus died on the cross.

Jesus was far from done fighting when His flesh died on the cross. Now in the spirit realm, the spirit of Jesus Christ descended into hell and defeated the devil in the devil's seat of power-hell!

Jesus Christ took from the devil the power of sin and death. Then the spirit of Jesus Christ returned to His earthly body that was then resurrected.

I could only imagine what all the players in the mock trial and crucifixion would say to Jesus' face after the resurrection. Pontius Pilate would surely urinate on himself. The entire Sanhedrin would fall on their face and grovel before Him, begging for mercy. King Herod (a different King Herod from the one who ordered all the male infants under three murdered thirty years previous) wanted to see Jesus perform a miracle; perhaps the king would save Jesus' life from the corrupt Sanhedrin if such a miracle was performed (Luke 23:8). I imagine Jesus appears before him after the resurrection, "You asked for a sign? See me now!"

For forty days, the resurrected Jesus Christ walked this earth. During that time, I don't know of any scriptural account involving the devil or his minions confronting Jesus. While these forty days played out, no effort was made in the furtherance of the evil one's agenda. Why not?

That tells me the devil conceded defeat. Like a politician admitting the loss of an election. As soon as the resurrected Christ ascended into heaven, the devil came back out against the creation. The players in the farce and sham of a trial and execution of Jesus Christ suddenly reappear to harass the apostles and the growing church.

That tells me the devil is picking his battles. It is a significant validation of the power of Jesus Christ. The devil won't even appear to confront Jesus Christ after the resurrection. As soon as Christ ascends back into heaven, the devil is out kicking down doors and persecuting people. What does that say to you?

My faith in Jesus Christ is bolstered by knowing this. I am also acutely aware that, for me, the devil is a very lethal opponent. Jesus Christ beat him, not me. I have to put *God* first and rely on *Him* to keep me safe from the devil's attempts to destroy me. I must be ever vigilant and exercise due diligence in my faith. I must have the proper attitude, will, and intent for continuing in my faith. If I slip, there is no doubt the devil will pounce. Let that serve as fair warning. Do not gloat or boast of the devil's failings; rather, praise Jesus Christ for His victory!

Even the archangel told the devil, "The Lord rebuke you" (Jude 1:9, BSB).

It is that reverence for the supreme power of God that displays our obedience to God. God will protect us. "For the eyes of the Lord roam to and fro over all the earth, to show Himself strong on behalf of those whose hearts are fully devoted to Him..." (2 Chronicles 16:9, BSB).

This scripture speaks to me voluminously. It is the one that motivated me enough to put all my thoughts into this work. God is looking to sponsor disciples of His Scripture. There is a very long induction process. A person must become familiar with the entire collection of inspired scripture. It is key to understand the history, people, places, and events that scripture describes.

Recognizing the scriptural and spiritual tools for what they are and learning how to employ them effectively is a labor of love. Such a person will have to make sacrifices that seem counterintuitive to worldly people.

The good news is the spiritual awareness broadens the understanding of life. The disciple of Scripture does not have it easier or enjoy any advantage over anyone else. It is the wisdom God imparts through a more accurate understanding of scripture that allows the disciple of it to make better decisions in life. God does the rest.

# Chapter 18

## How to Pray Like a Spiritual Ninja Warrior

## First, You Have to Believe

## I Mean Really Believe

I am reminded of a video of an event from June 6, 1989. It is of a man in Tiananmen Square, China, standing in front of a column of four military tanks. It is commonly referred to as "the tank guy video." Tank guy keeps moving his body into the path of the lead tank. He is preventing all four tanks from going where they want to.

Years ago, I was at work discussing this video with a coworker who said, "I wish I believed in something as much as tank guy believes in whatever he is standing in front of those tanks for!"

My question became, "How come some people just can't believe like tank guy?"

A lot of people say that they believe. In fact, they believe in everything the Bible says. The problem for them is they don't believe they can do what Jesus did.

My question then evolved into, "How can people be inspired to believe like tank guy?"

Scripture tells us that where two or more are gathered in Jesus' name, He is there. (Matthew 18:20). This makes the married couple a very potent prayer team. As the core of the family unit, a married couple can pray together in the company of Jesus Christ. He is everywhere at once. He is in both the husband's and the wife's hearts.

Believing that your Lord and Savior is present with you while you pray is empowering.

I want my readers to think about and imagine a married couple. Just starting out with a young child, a mortgage, car payments, and student loans on top of utilities, groceries, and a hectic work schedule. The husband is "papa bear." He is responsible to God for being a good steward and provider for his family. I would have to believe he would protect his family like "tank guy" was protecting whatever he was. If anyone else tries to meddle with his family, home, or livelihood, he is going to have righteous indignation on his side. He can stand his ground in faith and let the power of God flow through him into the world, and God's protections will surround him and his family, home, and career.

The wife is "mama bear." She is responsible to God for being a good steward and provider for her family. I believe she would protect her family like "tank guy" was protecting whatever he was. Let anybody try to meddle with her family, home, or livelihood, and she will also have righteous indignation on her side. She can stand her ground in faith and let the power of God flow through her into the world. God's protections will surround her and her family, home, and career.

The young child is innocent and attended to by guardian angels. That means there is a divine presence warding off the enemy. When the parents pray together, and Jesus is also present, the guardian angel is bolstered. This is why the family unit is so strong. That is why families are under attack by the enemy. Any way to split the parents, any stressor that can be plucked to cause strife will be strummed by the enemy.

Human tendency is to blame those closest to self for our discomfort. That is the enemy working against us. People don't get married because they want to fight and make each other miserable all the time. When a marriage is under attack by the enemy, it tends to look like a battleground.

Either the married couple pulls together and battles the enemy with God on their side, or they turn away from God, blame each other for problems, and stubbornly defend the error between them. The enemy knows a house divided will fall (Mark 3:25). Everything from loneliness to financial stress, to irritable infants, to jealousy and coveting what others have, are strategies and tactics deployed by the enemy against the family unit.

If we don't know the facts of our spouse's situation on a certain day, and we imagine for them a scenario that angers us, then when we get home, we are looking for a conflict with them. This is the enemy driving wedges between spouses.

To combat this in faith, we must consider our spouse as our own flesh. Why would we imagine something untrue to inflict pain and suffering on our self? That is exactly what we do when we falsely accuse others. We look bad, we instigate hostilities, and we suffer for it. The enemy attacking us thinks it is hilarious. They enjoy the show and keep stoking the flames to see how far they can drive the married couple away from godly conduct.

If we put God first, we have faith, hope, and love for our spouse. We give them credit for being good stewards of our relationship by default. We appreciate their time, effort, and talents in making and building a home we share in happiness. We come home anticipating goodness; we smile, hug, and say something sweet. That is what the enemy hates. We should understand this is us winning the battle. Putting God first results in God blessing us with more than we can imagine.

## Second, You Have to Be Inspired

We are not supposed to see our position in life, wealth, or the stuff and things we have as more important than our faith or people in general. When we think on a scale of the entire universe, it makes one galaxy seem insignificant. God created the entire universe out of nothingness. For Him, it was a day's work.

He wants us to love *Him* out of our own free will. *He* promises us if we are obedient to *Him*, there is no limit to what we can accomplish! In that sense of things, the entire universe is on the table. That is amazingly inspiring to me.

I am so inspired by it that I consider it when manifesting the physical assertion of faith in real life. What does that mean? What I mean by that is:

Number one is our biblical attitude. Every day we have a chance to let *God's* love and power flow through us. Does our attitude reflect our willingness to be a conduit for God's love to flow through us into the world?

Number two is our biblical willpower. Can we stick to what the Bible tells us even when it seems to contradict what we experience in real life? Does our willpower express our knowing and voluntary sacrifice of some earthly benefit or pleasure to accommodate *God's* will in our lives? Are we playing for eternity?

Number three is our intent to obtain a more accurate understanding of scripture. Do our intentions illustrate our faith through our words and deeds?

The attitude, will, and intent that we display in this world during our lifetime is what we will be judged by when we stand before God. Nobody likes to hear the boss say, "I don't like your attitude." How do we avoid hearing that? We apply ourselves fully to the boss's vision for us in their plan.

I try to make my attitude one of gratitude. I want to show myself thankful to God for making me perfect for my role in His plan. I try to apply my will to whatever *God's* plan is. His plan for us is going to come to pass. It just always seems to work out that way.

The most powerful prayer method is not based in a simple formula of words. It is founded in the proper biblical attitude, will, and intent. We have briefly discussed the attitude, will, and intent. Now I am going into the will part with a little more detail.

I used to think of "*God's* will" as a spiritual force that effected change in the physical world. Then I learned that through our faith in Jesus Christ, we are children of *God*. That makes us with Christ Jesus as our confessed *Lord* and Savior fellow heirs to eternal life!

Therefore the "will of *God*" becomes a legal promise, as in a last will and testament. Not a human estate planning tool but a scriptural promise from our Spiritual Father. We must know *God's* words do not return empty (Isaiah 55:11).

This promise is *God's* will for us in our lives and is our passport from existing as a fallen being on earth to becoming a forgiven soul in paradise with *God*. *God's* plan was for us to dwell with him in paradise. That was our "first estate." We sinned and are being punished for that sin.

Whether we know it or not, we are seeking to be reconciled back to God. Our drive to fill ourselves with happiness is God-seeking. When we are unfulfilled by stuff and things, we miss the point that God is waiting with His arms wide open for us to hug Him. Once we experience the peace that surpasses all understanding, we will not place so much value on our stuff and things (Philippians 4:7).

*God* has provided a way for us to get back into good standing with *Him*. That way is by our faith in Jesus Christ. Jesus told us that He is "the way, the truth, and the life" (John 14:6, KJV). If we have Jesus Christ in faith, we have *God's* will for us to become heirs to eternal life.

The willpower to see ourselves actualized into a state of good standing with *God* is the second ingredient for more powerful prayer. If we pray to win the lottery, does that work? No! Why not? Because it is not *God's* will for us to be materially wealthy at the expense of a condemned soul.

If we are rich in the soul, spiritually, we can be content with what we have. The desire for more things being above our desire to please *God* is the problem. It is a commandment, "You shall have no other gods before me" (Exodus 20:3, NIV).

The act of deferring to *God* as the giver of happiness but not letting Him be the source of your happiness is the problem. People want to ask, "What do I get from my faith?" It sounds silly to me. What do you get? How about eternal life in paradise? No more sickness, no more tears, no more pain or suffering, no more death. The only souls there with you are the same, faithful believers who chose to store up treasures in heaven rather than wealth on earth.

We will be restored to the plan *God* originally intended for us. The one from before Adam and Eve getting kicked out of the Garden of Eden for sinning against *God*. All the curses we now exist under and must endure will be lifted from us (Revelation 22:3). The peace that surpasses all understanding will be ours again (Philippians 4:7)!

We have discussed the attitude part and the will part. Now I am going to open on the intent part. *God's* original intent was for us to dwell in the Garden of Eden. The Garden of Eden was a paradise for human habitation. That has always been *God's* intent for us. We are the ones who took matters into our own hands and made a mess of things for ourselves.

People will argue, "If *God* is all-powerful and *He* created me with a plan *He* devised for my lifetime, how can I screw that up?" It is the built-in personal accountability for the exercise of our free will. *God* gave us free will. When we exercise our free will, we set in motion actions and reactions. What we have said or done triggers the natural consequences for ourselves and those around us.

*God* does not prevent us from using our free will because *He* wants us to choose to love *Him* of our own free will. If *He* controlled us and made us love *Him*, free will could not exist. We would be robots following a program we could not deviate from. If God wanted that, He would have done so. The evidence of our free will shows that God wants us to choose Him for our own reasons. The side effect of having free will is that we make mistakes, and we suffer the consequences for our mistakes. It is the natural order of things. We are supposed to learn from our mistakes.

I hear a lot of times, "Why does *God* let bad things happen to good people?" I can tell you that I have suffered many hurtful things in my life, some when I have done nothing wrong. Life wasn't all roses and champagne for our Lord and Savior either. Do you think Jesus being arrested in the middle of the night after Judas betrayed Him was a high point in His life?

If the Son of *God* suffered when He was here, what makes anybody else think they should not have to do so themselves? I was once told, "Existence is suffering." I disagreed at the time. I learned that it is true; however, every choice we make narrows our options in the future. Those limits begin to form barriers that exclude certain possibilities. Missed opportunity is a form of suffering. Like missing the opportunity to be saved and ending up condemned.

In a group environment or a society, the choices of other people also have an impact in our lives. *God* made a plan; then *He* put people with free will into the mix. Bad things happen because of bad choices made by people, not because *God* allows them. What *God* is teaching us is that *His* plan works best for us when we apply *His* rules to our ways.

All things work together for the glory of God (Romans 8:28). *God's* plan will be fulfilled. No matter what good people do. No matter what bad people do. *God* uses it all to bring about *His* will. It is our limited ability to recognize the possibilities that make things seem impossible to us.

Knowing *God* can do anything is inspiring. Believing in faith that we can be the conduit through which *God's* love and power flow into this world is fantastic! If we are one of those conduits, we participate in *God's* will being done. From believing to being blessed to becoming a blessing to others, awesome! This is only possible with a more accurate understanding of scripture and applying it to our attitude, will, and intent every day.

### Third, Know What You Are Seeing

I call it the difference between "spiritual eyes" and "worldly eyes." With "worldly eyes," we look upon things as more important to our happiness. With "spiritual eyes," we see that our faith is our happiness.

As I said above, this doesn't mean the only thing we have is our faith. What I am saying is a person needs to put *God* first in faith. If we do that, then *God* will bless us with more stuff. The idea is we are to be a blessing to others because of our stuff.

I describe it this way. Looking through "spiritual eyes," we see that: *God* created all things. He may have used human hands to make a lot of what we are familiar with. *God* made us in *His* image. *He* is the original "*Creator*." Humans like to create at our level. We don't make things out of nothing like *God*. We modify some raw materials into something we want. We fabricate; the Lord creates.

Bearing that in mind, everything is *God's*. We may possess it for a lifetime, but *God* is its keeper forever. Therefore, if we allow ourselves to become the "conduit" for *God's* work to flow through us into our world, the side effect is we benefit from our participation in "*God's* will be done...")

Looking through "worldly eyes," we see that: I have done the work. I earned what I have. Nobody helped me. This is all mine. Nobody else can tell me what to do with it. If I want it to sit on a shelf and gather dust, that is my business.

Bearing that in mind, everything we have, our stuff, and things become god to us. We see other people as the problem. They want our stuff. We become defensive and overprotective of our stuff. Therefore, we are closed off to *God* and become our own stumbling block in faith. The side effect is we get farther away from *God* in heaven with every new god of stuff and things we own on earth.

Jesus said it Himself when *He* walked this earth, "What sorrow awaits you who are rich, for you have your only happiness now" (Luke 6:24, NLT).

By putting stuff above people, we deny the greatness of *God's* creation, that is, us. *God's* plan is for us to be reconciled back to *Him* in paradise forever. To see that, we need to look through our "spiritual eyes." Can we afford to "look the other way"?

If you really believe you are inspired with the proper biblical attitude, will, and intent, and you are looking through your "spiritual eyes," *God* will reveal a great many things to you. It is written that when we experience such revelation from *God* and see the scriptures playing out before us, we are to consider ourselves blessed indeed (Psalm 89:15).

I was getting ready to leave the house for a long day. I got a shiver, and that little voice in my head said, "Take an umbrella with you." I stopped what I was doing and went outside. I looked at the sky. I saw blue sky in every direction. I told myself, "*I don't need an umbrella.*" I left the house for the day without an umbrella.

Imagine my dismay only eight hours later when I was getting heavily rained on. If I had an umbrella, I could have stayed dry. That shiver got me again. I think that little voice in my head said, "*Should have listened to me.*"

There are other experiences like that. I simply learned to listen to that voice or pay the price for ignoring it. There was a time I impulsively grabbed an item the little voice told me I needed. I had it with me. Literally had forgotten I even had it. Then a situation came up; that item was exactly what was needed for the solution. Then I get that shiver and a warm feeling. Is it a reward for listening? I think so.

Many times, I have run into people who conduct themselves in a manner that I do not consider scripturally accurate. I don't treat them differently than anyone else. I give them the same opportunity to prove themselves as I give everyone else. I feel that spiritual impression telling me to be on my guard.

I have interacted with such people asking God to take control of the situation. There have been times I accidentally discovered the person in question talking bad about me behind my back. I have had such people try to bully me. I have heard plenty of tough luck stories. The classic damsel in distress scenario comes up often.

How does one discern if the person is a genuine believer in scripture or just playing such to increase their take on a hustle?

It can be very tough to tell. One thing for certain is if you tell the person no one time and they quit asking you, you can bet it was just a hustle. If you say no the first time and they try to help you, that is a strong indication that they are genuine.

I once saw a panhandler with a sign that read, "Need money for beer research." I thought that was clever enough and honest enough to give him enough money for a drink.

I have also been approached by an obvious hustler in very fine dress who laid out a long story about trying to get home to help his aged mother, and he only needed a little gas money to make it. I saw his Mercedes Benz and said, "I could use some gas money too." He smiled and winked as he went on his way. "It never hurts to ask," he said.

You never know for sure, but you can take stock of the environment and circumstances.

# Chapter 19

## What a Christian Does Is

## Knowing—Praying—Heaping—Storing

What kind of list is that? The list of the necessary fundamentals for meaningful scripture-based faith. Our existence, whether we asked to exist or not, places us firmly on the battlefield between obedience and disobedience to God.

Being obedient to God is the way we receive blessing from God. If we are disobedient to God, we invite God's curses upon us. This stuff is real; I see it working both ways. If we see it working, that is a sign from God that we are seeing with our spiritual eyes. It will not make sense to the worldly. Identifying that inability of the worldly to "*get it*" is further confirmation that scripture is playing out before our spiritual eyes. (We will know them by their fruit, Matthew 7:16.)

What will we know?

Knowing is knowing the scriptures. Understanding what the Holy Bible does say. Having the wisdom to apply that knowledge in our daily life of faith.

*Knowing...*

...is not just reading the Bible once, a long time ago, when you were younger. Knowing is a lifelong process. Read a chapter every day. Read through the whole Bible over time. Start reading the Bible over again every time you finish it. The purpose is to have a more accurate and intimately personal understanding of how the scriptures really do intertwine with everything in human existence every day and every way.

Every time I read the Bible again, I pick up new things that I don't remember being there in any of my previous readings of the Bible. It depends on what is happening in my life at the time and what new insight I get from my continued reading and rereading of the Holy Bible. No other book is that way for me.

I have also come to believe that each scripture has a meaning for the physical human existence, the spiritual realm, and has a historical/future reference.

With that in mind, while reading, there are many levels of meaning in scripture, and all work together to reveal more about the human mission in *God's* eternal plan.

It is these deeper meanings that draw my mind to ponder. Reflecting on the scripture, "[...] were not our hearts burning within us as He spoke with us on the road and opened the Scriptures to us?" (Luke 24:32, BSB)

I call this the mana of scripture, more potent than both the milk and the meat of scripture.

It is this deeper meaning and the many ways it can be viewed, depending on personal point of view and where one is at in their life cycle, which are the rich soil to plant the seeds of our prayers.

Praying

I reflect when I pray: what else can I draw from this scripture to help me in my walk? How does this scripture benefit from the context of the chapter it is in? What about the book it is from and then the whole Bible? What is it that God wants me to know?

"Life and death are in the power of the tongue, and those who love it will eat its fruit" (Proverbs 18:21, BSB).

These prayers illicit a response from the Holy Spirit dwelling in us. That little voice of our spirit talks to us. We can listen to or ignore it.

Praying is to pray the way *God* tells us works best for us once we have a firm grasp on the knowing part.

"[...] The prayer of a righteous man has great power to prevail" (James 5:16, BSB).

True believers faithful to biblical scripture will gain a more accurate and intimate personal understanding of the scriptures in the Holy Bible through the Holy Spirit. When praying in the spirit, believers can pray very powerful prayers. Once a prayer warrior has had their say in prayer, it is important to know they must wait ever so patiently on *God* to do *His* work in *His* time.

"[...] Blessed are all who wait for Him" (Isaiah 30:18, BSB).

Some examples of very powerful prayers follow:

Pray, "In the name of Jesus Christ, the willing ransom for all man's sins, so that we may be reconciled back to God, forgive me for all my sins, iniquities, transgressions, and backslidings. Wash me with the blood of Jesus Christ, find me without blemish blameless in Your sight, fill me with the Holy Spirit, and hear my prayer. By the power of Jesus' resurrection, ascension, and promised return in victory, according to Your will, in Your time, You know what I need, bless me with Your undeserved loving-kindness, grace, and mercy."

Pray, "I understand that Satan is an overwhelming adversary for me, but I also know I find salvation in You through faith in Your Son, Father *God*. Therefore, I am as helpless as a child in an evil jungle full of Satan's enmity toward me and all who love You, Father *God*. Also, I am at great peril and jeopardy to all of Satan's minions, the forces that obey Satan, and those who serve Satan for the purpose of my destruction and the destruction of all those who love You, Father

*God*. Likewise, I pray for Your almighty, all-knowing, everywhere at once in all times protection against all that is evil and against You, Father God, and against all who love You, Father *God*."

Pray, "Father *God*, let it be Your will, in the name of Jesus Christ, Your Son, Your invincible powers protect us and keep us safe from all harm."

Pray, "Father *God*, let it be Your will, in the name of Jesus Christ, Your Son, Your hedge of protection surrounds us, our property, and possessions so that the evil one and his minions may not cause us any spiritual, physical, personal, mental, emotional, or financial hardship."

Pray, "Father *God*, You know the evil we face and what we stand to lose by failing in our faith. Give us the information, knowledge, understanding, wisdom, deliberative capacity, discernment, and sagacity we need to maintain our refuge in You and achieve the faith You desire in us."

Pray, "Father *God*, let us be positive, encouraging, and uplifting."

Pray, "Father *God*, let me be a contributor to the advancement of Your interests on earth in my lifetime."

Pray, "Father *God*, allow my effort to praise and glorify You and allow me to enjoy it myself."

Pray, "Father *God*, may You allow my efforts to store up treasures in heaven."

Pray, "Father *God*, may You allow my efforts to heap coals upon those who hate You."

Pray, "Father *God*, may You allow my efforts to heap coals upon those who hate Your people."

Pray, "Father *God*, may it be Your will, in the name of your Son, Jesus Christ, my *Lord* and Savior, in, with, and through the Holy

Spirit, that my efforts in the advancement of Your interests on earth mightily prick the hearts of those who practice vice, the things You hate and partake of the fruits of the vineyard of the wicked."

Pray, "Father *God*, may it be Your will, in the name of Jesus Christ, Your Son, and my *Lord* and Savior, that my efforts in the advancement of Your interests on earth be a legacy for all Christians."

Pray, "Jesus Christ, the only-begotten Son of Father *God* almighty, my *Lord* and Savior, as You pray for me, by the power of Your resurrection, ascension, and prophesied return in victory, by the power of the Holy Spirit, may it be the Father's will to save us from ourselves."

Pray, "Jesus Christ, save us from what we do not know."

Pray, "Jesus Christ, thank You for all that You have done for me. All the praise, honor, glory, thanks, and dominion are Yours forever and ever, and I praise and worship You for Your willing sacrifice for the redemption of all sinners."

Pray, "Father *God*, I ask You for Your will to be done in my life."

Pray, "Father *God*, I thank You in the name of Jesus Christ, my *Lord* and Savior."

Pray, "Father *God*, Your ways are higher than mine, if I have erred in any way, please forgive me with Your undeserved loving-kindness, grace, and mercy, and I pray that You make things right and just according to Your will and in the name of Jesus Christ, my *Lord* and Savior."

Pray, "By the pain, suffering, and blood willingly shed by Jesus Christ for the redemption of all sinners."

Pray, "I believe in Father *God*, Jesus Christ, the Son, and the Holy Ghost."

Pray, "I believe the Three are One, and each One is all Three."

Pray, "Father *God*, almighty, all-knowing, all-powerful, everywhere at once in all times."

Pray, "I believe the Holy Bible scriptures are Your words to me, Father *God*."

Pray, "I have been baptized with the water, washed in the blood of Jesus Christ, filled with the Holy Spirit, all my sins are washed away, I have been redeemed."

Pray, "Thank You, Father *God*, for all the blessing You have bestowed upon us, all the blessing we are enjoying, and all the blessing You will bestow upon us."

Pray, "Father *God*, You know what we need; bless us with all the blessings You can bestow upon us."

Pray, "Father *God*, let Your blessing rain down on us continually."

Pray, "Father *God*, lead us, guide us, protect us, make our way straight, flat, and level before us."

When we pray like this, we will "heap burning coals on his [the enemy's] head, and the LORD will reward you [us]" (Proverbs 25:22, NIV).

Heaping is the spiritual "heaping of coals" on those wolves in sheep's clothing, nonbelievers (and worse, the anti-Christians) who see fit to try and take advantage of the true Christians who are faithful to the scriptures of the Holy Bible.

*Heaping*

When *God* exercises His divine judgment upon sinners, true believers faithful to biblical scripture will see it and receive it with sorrow. The sinner's punishment is an awful price to pay. We pity the sinner that refuses to turn from their bad behavior and embrace Jesus Christ.

Why would a believer faithful to Bible scripture feel sorrow for a sinner punished by *God*? Because the scriptures tell us that *God* does not glory in the perishing of sinners but in the redemption of them (Ezekiel 18:32). That is overcoming evil with *good*. As spiritual ambassadors, we are to pray for the correction of bad behavior and the redemption of the sinner. Our example is supposed to show that by following the law of God, through our obedience to it, life is better for us. The wise will see that it is so, and the seed of faith will be planted in them. God can then work in them. In our modern society, the people faithful to biblical scripture do not value money, power, or privilege above other people. Not even sinners. We pray for all to come to know *God, Jesus Christ*, and *the Holy Spirit*! We loath the sin but love the sinner, just as Jesus Christ did.

When we know, pray, and heap, we also store. Storing is the storing up of treasures in heaven for yourself that will last you for all eternity. No eye has seen, no ear has heard, no heart has imagined what the *Lord* has prepared for those who love *Him* (1 Corinthians 2:9).

I get truly uplifted by meditating on that scripture. *God* made us, and He has prepared a place for us. In that place, He has given us a great abundance we cannot even imagine. All the people throughout all human history who are saved by the grace of *God* will be in that place. Not a single person who fails *God's* test will be there. I have a great hope for attaining such an existence by the grace of *God*.

*Storing*

A personal relationship with *God* starts through daily reading of the Bible and praying to Him about everything that concerns us. I pray to God as if speaking to my most trusted and powerful ally. I am as honest as I can be. I fear only provoking God's wrath on me.

An intimate knowledge of *God's* scriptures in the Holy Bible, yes, Old and New Testaments, is essential. I use scripture in my prayers. It is written, *the scripture I am meditating on*, God, please edify me.

By enacting a personal model of behavior taken from the example of Jesus Christ. By seeking to display the attributes Jesus exhibited, we are told in scripture to attain them, and by simultaneously avoiding the characteristics we are told in scripture to avoid. (Always refer to scripture.) We begin and continue a lifelong process of storing up treasures with our eternal Father in heaven above.

It is literally "*God*-given treasure" to us personally. No moth will eat anything, no rust will destroy anything, and no thief can steal anything when it is given to us by *God* in heaven (Matthew 6:20).

We know we are born into this world naked, and naked we will go from this world, unable to take anything with us that we accumulated during our lives. Really what is the point to gathering up huge quantities of wealth, power, and prestige if none of it will follow us into the ever after? It is all stuff that will weigh us down into the fiery furnace where there is much wailing and gnashing of teeth. Is that the goal of our earthly existence? No! Eternal life in paradise with *God* is.

We can take from the example of the ancient Pharaohs' tombs. All the stuff that was meant to accompany them into the afterlife is still here on earth. Some is in museums around the world, some in private collections. The point is no matter how carefully it is planned out, the stuff remains after we have gone beyond.

If an Egyptian Pharaoh with all the rites and rituals of mummification ends up leaving his stuff behind, that should tell us something. "You can't take it with you!" I like to think it is because what is in heaven is so much better!

I am a space nut. I grew up watching Captain Kirk travel to different star systems and land on different planets. I love cosmology and long to be able to see up close all that God has made. I imagine this would be heaven. I know it will take eons, but what else is there to do for eternity? See what God has made and appreciate it with awe and wonder.

# Chapter 20

## HUMBLE YOURSELF

We are humans. Humans have limitations. We are foolish to our own detriment if we exceed our limitations. Not even the archangel defied Satan to his face. The archangel very humbly told Satan, "The LORD rebuke you" (Jude 1:9, NIV).

Be humble; rely completely on *God*, who defeated the devil a dozen times already. Put your faith and trust in the Victorious Christ Jesus. Let *Him* be your everything, your all in all (1 Corinthians 15:28).

When Satan comes calling. When false prophets speak. When the principalities and powers of the air are aligned against you. When temptation attacks you, be humble in yourself. Call upon the most powerful name we know, the name of *Jesus Christ*!

Read the Bible every day. When you get to the end, start over. Live your life in accordance with all that you understand the Holy Bible to say. Pray to *God* every day for all things that are on your mind and in your heart. Give thanks to *God* for the good in your life. Be a blessing to other *God*-fearing people if you can. Do not foolishly let unbelievers overcome your goodness with their evil. Do your best to always overcome evil with good. Be ever weary of the anti-Christian movement. They are working against us 24/7/365. Know that God has got this! Praise the *Lord*!

### OF ESTATES, PRINCIPALITIES, AND POWERS OF THE HEIR

The first estate of human existence was in the Garden of Eden. The Garden of Eden was perfect for human habitation. That is where

*God* put us. That is where *God* meant for us to be. That is where *God* intended for us to stay, forever. We were immortal before the fall.

We gave up our first estate by committing sin. We lost our paradise and the opportunity to commune with *God*. Our new residence, the earth, was cursed. Man was cursed. Woman was cursed. The serpent was cursed.

Ever since, humankind has failed many times. You can be sure that the enemy was deeply intrenched in the events leading up to such failures. After Adam and Eve were evicted from the Garden of Eden, their son Cain killed their son Able. That brought the curse of the mark upon Cain.

There was the curse at the tower of Babel where *God* confused the language of men.

There are the blessings for obedience to *God*. There are the curses for disobedience to *God*. These came soon after the Israelites were led out of bondage in Egypt.

In our current estate of human existence, we have a great deal of curses to overcome. If that wasn't challenging enough, we would enjoy an added degree of difficulty. The additional challenge is an intelligent force trying to cause us to fail. It is not only Satan by himself but all his minions. Literally one-third of the host of heaven (Revelation 12:4).

The principalities are intangible spiritual sovereigns. They are all evil. There is one for each vice, a.k.a. the seven deadly sins.

Greed (1 Timothy 6:10).

Sloth (Ecclesiastes 10:18).

Wrath (Romans 12:19).

Gluttony (Proverbs 23:19–20).

Lust (Matthew 5:28).

Envy (Job 5:2).

Pride (Proverbs 16:18).

For each vice, there is a virtue to overcome it with Good.

Charity is the counter to greed. (See Philippians 2:3.)
Diligence is the counter to slothfulness. (See Galatians 6:9.)
Patience is the counter to wrath. (See Psalm 37:8–9.)
Temperance is the counter to gluttony. (See Proverbs 25:16.)
Chastity is the counter to lust. (See 1 Corinthians 6:18.)
Contentedness is the counter to envy. (See Proverbs 23:17.)
Humility is the counter to pride. (See James 4:6.)

When we are tempted by a vice, we call upon the virtue that counters it. This propels the Holy Spirit and God's warring angels into the fight ahead of us. We must stand firm and resist the devil; then, he will flee. Not because he is worried about us, but because we have set the holy host of heaven on his heels. He knows he has lost. He relies on trickery and deception to get us to trip ourselves up. Only we can turn away from God and thereby lose God's protection.

The enemy is expert at instigating our bad behavior. He offers us a skewed view of our circumstances. He wants us to consider things we know are wrong. Once we allow that thought process to begin, we can convince ourselves that we have no other choice. It is our free will to decide what words we will speak and which actions we will take that the enemy leverages toward the darkness. He wants to steal your soul, don't give the thief a chance.

There is another principality for each of the things that *God* hates:

1. "a proud look,

2. a lying tongue,

3. hands that shed innocent blood,

4. a heart that devises wicked plans,

5. feet that are swift in running to evil,

6. a false witness who speaks lies,

7. and one who sows discord among brethren."[3]

"To fear the Lord is to hate evil; I hate arrogant pride, evil conduct, and perverse speech" (Proverbs 8:13, BSB).

For all that *God* hates, there is a love that overcomes them.

"And now these three remain: faith, hope, and love; but the greatest of these is love" (1 Corinthians 13:13, BSB).

"Jesus declared, 'Love the Lord your God with all your heart and with all your soul and with all your mind.' This is the first and greatest commandment. And the second is like it: 'Love your neighbor as yourself'" (Matthew 22:37–39, BSB).

"But the fruit of the Spirit is love, joy, peace, patience, kindness, goodness, faithfulness, gentleness, and self-control. Against such things there is no law" (Galatians 5:22–23, BSB).

3      (paraphrased) Proverbs 6:17–19, KJV

*Love is patient, love is kind. It does not envy, it does not boast, it is not proud. It is not rude, it is not self-seeking, it is not easily angered, it keeps no account of wrongs. Love takes no pleasure in evil, but rejoices in the truth. It bears all things, believes all things, hopes all things, endures all things.*

1 Corinthians 13:4–7 (BSB)

When we are faced with hatred burning in us, we counter it with love. When we pray to God to quench the hate we feel with His love, the enemy will have to flee. They do recall the defeat they suffered during the war in heaven. They see the victorious holy host of heaven loosed against them by our plea to our Creator for His help.

It is like the younger sibling fighting a bully elder sibling. When the younger sibling calls for help, his father will come. The bully knows he is lost and runs away. The bully looks for easy prey. The enemy is the same way. The fallen angels pick their battles. When you are weak, when the pressure is building on you, and your focus is on other things and not God, they ambush you. When you recognize the attack, that is when you must call in reinforcements.

I read in Job the term "the vineyard of the wicked" (Job 24:6, NIV).

As I prayed and meditated on that term later, my mind wandered. If the fruits of the spirit (Galatians 5:22–23) were from God, then where were the fruits of the vineyard of the wicked from?

Like virtues are to vice, so the fruits of the spirit are to the vineyard of the wicked.

173

*Fruit of the Spirit Vineyard of the Wicked*
(Galatians 5:22–23) (opposite of fruit of the spirit)

| | |
|---|---|
| Love | Enmity |
| Joy | Anxiety |
| Peace | Conflict |
| Patience | Haste |
| Gentleness | Viciousness |
| Goodness | Wickedness |
| Faith | Doubt |
| Meekness | Recklessness |
| Self-Control | Unruly |

Armed with this new counter to fight the devil's tactics against me, with the grace of God working through me, I was better prepared to resist the adversary and his more onerous deceptions.

We hope for salvation against all that is aligned against us. Be stubborn in your faith. Know that you will get knocked down from time to time. Every time you are knocked down, get back up, dust yourself off, and praise the *Lord* (Proverbs 24:16)!

For the estates and principalities will one day pass away. But the word of the Heir, Jesus Christ, will endure forever (1 Peter 1:25). It is Jesus Christ who has defeated every enemy. Jesus Christ is the one offering us a share in His victory. All we have to do to attain it is put *God* first in our life. Play the game of life with our eyes on the prize of eternal life with *God* in paradise. Our eternal treasure will be there waiting for us. Play for eternity!

*God* bless you with all the blessing that *He* can bestow upon you!

When new believers begin the adventure of faith, they are spiritual infants and require spiritual milk from scripture. They are still learning the chronology, people, places, and events that make up scripture. It is confusing and may seem contradictory to the beginner.

As a believer grows stronger in the competence of their scriptural vocabulary, they understand the chronology, people, places, and events described in scripture. They can use it to guide their path in their walk. This is the meat of the scripture. As mature Christians, the scripture is the solid food that sustains our faith.

When our life circumstances begin to grow more complex and intricate, we seek the deeper meanings of scripture. This is the mana of scripture. We know who wrote the book, who they wrote it to, what it meant to them at the time, and how it can be applied today. We study the words in Latin and Greek. We explore the Bible commentaries. We can also reference other scriptures, different historical periods, and how the scripture was important to those people in that place and at that time.

The mana of the scripture can be seen from the points of view of the poor, the prince, the priest, and the prophet. The good steward can apply the scripture to physical, mental, emotional, and spiritual aspects of life, from infants to great grandparents. At this stage of our spiritual walk, there is little that can draw us away from God. We have learned to trust Him. We follow scriptures without doubt or hesitation. It leaves very little ground for the enemy to gain a foothold. We are told not to give the enemy any footholds (Ephesians 4:27).

We are told to put on the full armor of God:

> *[...] with the belt of truth buckled around your waist, with the breastplate of righteousness arrayed, with your feet fitted with the readiness of the gospel of peace. In addition to all this, take up the shield of faith, with which you can extinguish all the flaming arrows of the evil one. And take the helmet of salvation and the sword of the Spirit, which is the word of God.*

Ephesians 6:14–17 (BSB)

While we are prepared for battle in this manner, we are also told: "Pray in the Spirit at all times, with every kind of prayer and petition" (Ephesians 6:18, BSB).

This is our scriptural warrior persona. Like a Roman soldier in the time of Christ. Physical life is ever-changing, always evolving, and the escalation of tactics between those obedient to God and those who are disobedient to God is literally a spiritual arms race. To go along with the spiritual milk, meat, and mana, the *enemy* deploys what I call the sourers of milk, the spoilers of meat, and the fermenters of mana.

When a person first learns "the Good News," they are said to be "infants in their faith" and receive the "milk" of the word of *God*. As a person grows in faith, they become adolescents in faith, able to take the "meat" of the word of *God*. Once a person is established in their faith as a way of life, they become adults in faith. Adults in faith can take the "mana" from scriptures. That is the opening of the scriptures as a blessing from heaven. Seeing how the scriptures can be applied to our physical life, mental, emotional, and spiritual existence in several life circumstances.

In summary, there is the milk, meat, and mana of scripture-based faith.

To combat the scripturally faithful person in each stage of their development, the devil has devised a series of attacks. For those new to the faith who are receiving the "milk" of the faith, Satan attacks with what I call the "sourers of the milk."

These sourers of the milk come in the forms of doubt, fear, distraction, and selfish pursuits.

For those trying to grow their faith by taking the meat, Satan attacks with what I call the spoilers of the meat. The spoilers of the meat come in the forms of chaotic time constraints, faith negative obligations, false reports, and the letter of the law being used to defeat the spirit of the law.

For those who have established their faith as a way of life and are sustained by the mana, Satan attacks them with what I call the fermenters of mana. The fermenters of mana come in the forms of the stumbling block, stifling spirits, temptation, and a wrongfully disposed heart (in others).

In summary, the devil opposes our faith with the sourers of milk, spoilers of meat, and the fermenters of mana.

Our reality is we are sinners who exist in a fallen state. We have been cursed; our world has been cursed. There is an intelligent force working against us. The army of darkness. They possess enmity toward us. Enmity is worse than hate; it is a kill on sight kind of prejudice. We must realize this to know what we are truly up against. Every step in our journey of faith is contested by at least a minion of evil. More often, we are being attacked by many minions of evil.

We have been given the tools to combat the evils we face. For each vice, there is a virtue. For each of the things that *God* hates, there is something that *God* loves. For each fruit of the vineyard of the wicked, there is a fruit of the spirit. We are equipped with armor and a weapon.

Knowing what we are up against is helpful but knowing how to fight back is *divine*. Use scripture to formulate your way and your defenses. This war is for real, and losing it lasts forever, the same as winning it.

This spiritual war is a lifelong condition. As our life progresses, so do our challenges. As we become better equipped to resist the enemy, the enemy ups his game. There is the bait and switch tactic that Satan loves to use against us.

We are led to believe a situation is one vice, hate, or fruit of the vineyard of the wicked, so we prepare for that. Then when we confront the situation, it is something else. We are unprepared and must immediately reevaluate and deploy the correct defense.

These things happen in combat. We must be quick to see things changing and adapt to them on the fly. There is no place for doubt, fear, distraction, or selfish pursuits. Such things are the weapons of the enemy.

Our defense is standing firm, trusting in the Lord, maintaining our focus, and humbling ourselves. When we do those things in obedience to God, He is the one who fights for us. When He does, we are to give Him all the praise, honor, glory, and our thanks.

We should never gloat (Proverbs 24:17–18). We are powerless without God. Gloating over the vanquished foe is an invitation to potent delusion and certain suffering. Gloating is pride. Pride comes before a fall. Don't set yourself up for failure. Our words give power to spiritual forces. Try your best to be positive, encouraging, and uplifting. Those things we can stand having power in our lives.

# Chapter 21

## Putting It All Together

When Jesus Christ walked this earth, His homeland was under Roman occupation. At that time, the Roman legions were the most powerful army on the planet. The Praetorian Guard was like the secret service and special operations combined. The Romans also had a very strong navy. They were learned and an economic powerhouse as well.

Roman soldiers wore the best armor, carried the best weapons, had the best training, and employed battle-proven strategies and tactics. It was only rational thinking to respect their power and not deliberately oppose them.

Scriptures refer to weapons of warfare to make their point vivid. It would be easy for an unarmed citizen unhappy with the Roman occupation to get frustrated and get into trouble.

Jesus didn't teach rebellion or physical war. He talked about spiritual righteousness and letting *God* go before the believer. Waiting upon the Lord meant certain blessings. I picture the Israelites receiving the promised land. *God* went out before them and concurred the enemy. The fighting men of the Israelites mopped up behind *God* (Deuteronomy 9:3).

I don't know where the enemy, the evil one, is hiding, but *God* does. I want to pray powerfully enough to obliterate the devil's forces aligned against me. I want to pray smart enough to allow *God* to interpret my prayers so they can accomplish their mission according to *God's* will.

*God* knows! He can send in the warring angels He created for that specific purpose. *He* can drop them in right where they are needed at the second they are needed. *He* can anticipate when and where they will be needed so they are in place when the devil attempts his evil. Immediate smackdown! Before anything bad happens.

I have listed in the "Bibliography" a website (the last site listed) that highlights scriptures for our warring angels. I am a believer in them. Knowing when I pray that I am asking *God* to send out *His* warring angels before me is reassuring. Isaiah 54:17, Psalm 34:7, and Psalm 44:5 are my favorites!

When we close our prayers, we customarily say "amen"! Or when we agree with a statement or as a witness to another believer who has evoked a scripture. It means, "So be it," we have said our part; now we wait for *God* to bring it about. *God* hears us, and in *His* time, He answers, but we might not recognize the answer received as what we meant to ask for.

That is why I say, "You can give people exactly what they ask for, and they still don't have what they want." For a person to get what they need requires an inner reflection on what they really need versus what they just want. Our wants sometimes overcome our needs. If we have prayed our best prayer, meeting all the conditions set out in scripture, and allow *God* to interpret our prayer to accommodate *His* will, look out, world! Amen.

May *God* bless you with all the blessings that *He* can bestow upon you.

## THE HOLY SPIRIT

Jesus told the apostles that He would send us an Advocate (John 14:16). This Advocate, the Holy Spirit, is our comforter in place of Jesus. The Holy Spirit is often compared to water. Water is a very anomalous element compared to the rest of the liquids that are found on earth. There are over forty anomalies in water when compared to other liquids. Some people have suggested to me that water was not specifically created by God in the scriptures (Genesis 1:2). I think it is fitting that the Holy Spirit is compared to such an element. It was with God before the creation of light, while the heavens and the earth were formless and void.

The one difference between water and the Holy Spirit is that water always takes the path of least resistance. The Holy Spirit is often the energy that is effecting change in our world.

God's creation, humankind, is made of as much as 70 percent water. The recipe for humans is water, the dust of the earth, and the breath of life from God. It may be the anomalies in water that help account for all the variance in humankind. Like snowflakes, no two of us are exactly the same. Maybe identical twins come close, but even they become less identical as they grow and develop their own likes, dislikes, and circles of friends.

On the Gaia network, I watched a documentary on water. It is titled *Secret of Water, Discover the Language of Life*. In this documentary, a Japanese researcher, Masaru Emoto, conducted fifteen years of research on water crystals. They found that healthy water produced beautiful, hexagonal crystals like snowflakes when frozen. Unhealthy water could barely produce a hexagonal crystal. The experiments this researcher did with water showed that water samples from the same bucket of source water reacted positively to positive attention and negatively to negative attention. This research found that water reacted the worst to being ignored.

It made me wonder if people are 70 percent water, could we separate the water from our blood and freeze the water portion to see what kind of crystals formed in it? What would that tell us about the person it came from? Good crystal—good person? Bad crystal—bad person? We are told to avoid the blood (Leviticus 17:10–12). It might be better that we don't know.

I encourage everyone reading this to not confine God, Jesus Christ, or the Holy Spirit to a box we can comprehend. They are so much larger than we can possibly grasp. It will become clear to us in time that this is true. For believers, this is an amazing way to live. For those who would rather not indulge, it leaves a certain mystery of the universe. For those anti-Christians, this is probably the scariest thing you know of next to scripture itself.

There is no safe zone between the spiritual forces of light and darkness (Matthew 12:30). The war is raging all around us, whether we believe in it or not. There is only obedience or disobedience (Proverbs 6:20–22). Instead of trying to find the loopholes in the law, we should simply be obedient to the law. Hell is never full (Proverbs 30:15–16).

If you don't learn, you will burn.

"[...] The LORD will withhold no good thing from those who do what is right" (Psalm 84:11b, NLT).

Are you all *bright*? A measure of how on fire you are for the *Lord*! May God bless you with all the blessings that He can bestow upon you.

## DREAMING

While researching the scriptures for the section on virtue, I grew weary and nodded off. While I was sleeping, I had the following vision:

In my vision, I saw a man with nothing more to give. The man was naked, and his dirty face was tear-stained. An angel of the Lord appeared to him. They conferred briefly. The angel of the Lord asked the man, "Why are you naked and so sad?" Waiving his hand around him to bring attention to the many poor and needy, the man replied, "There are so many in need. There is nothing more that I can give to comfort them." The angel of the Lord asked the man, "Do you believe that Jesus Christ is the only-begotten Son of *God*?" The man nodded. The angel of the Lord reached inside his own chest. He grabbed ahold of something. When he retrieved his hand, there was a small orb in his hand. It shone like a miniature sun. The angel of the Lord pressed the glowing orb into the man's chest. The man was suddenly overcome with an abundance of riches. The man smiled and thanked the angel in the name of Jesus Christ. As I watched, the man departed from the angel. I saw the angel also watched the man as he went.

When people came to the man who had received the gift, he gave to them in abundance. Each one he gave to became burdened with great wealth. They, too, began giving away their wealth. In time many people burdened by great wealth returned to the angel.

The men of much wealth were in a circle around the angel. All spoke in one voice, "We give and give until we can find no one in need. Still, our blessings flow. We want to give back to the Lord who sent you. We return a portion of our blessing today for all the future generations to receive also."

Each man held out his hands toward the angel of the Lord. From each man, a river of wealth flowed toward the angel. The angel was encircled by twelve rivers of wealth flowing into his being.

Looking toward heaven, the angel said, "To whom was given, they have gifted back out of their blessing."

Then I heard a voice from above, "To these generous men, I will bless their children and their children's children to the seventh generation."

After that, I woke up with a start.

In this world, with worldly people, it is possible to give someone exactly what they ask for; and they will not have what they want. A person's stuff and things cannot fill the lack when it is Jesus Christ that is missing from their heart. The river of wealth flowing from the giver to the receiver is the more accurate understanding of scripture and God. It is the treasure stored up in heaven. It is "catchy" and can be passed from one believer to another. It is true: to receive, you must give. Like many things in scripture, the way things really work is opposite to the way we see them working in the world between worldly people. The world reflects heaven above, upside down, and backward from what the Lord intended. As a disciple of Scripture, the unconditional love of our Lord and Savior flows through us into the world. We call attention to the things that people do not know are hurting them. We do this so they can avoid needless pain, shame, and guilt. We love to help people in this way. May God bless all disciples of Scripture with all the blessings that He can bestow upon them. Amen!

# BIBLIOGRAPHY

*Books:*

Stedman, R. C. *Adventuring Through the Bible*. Grand Rapids, Michigan: Discovery House Publishers.

Strong, J. A. LL.D., S.T.D. *The New Strong's Exhaustive Concordance of the Bible: With Main Concordance, Appendix to the Main Concordance, Hebrew and Aramaic Dictionary of the Old Testament, Greek Dictionary of the New Testament*. Thomas Nelson Publishers, Nashville, Atlanta, London, Vancouver.

*The Lost Books of the Bible and the Forgotten Books of Eden*. Cleveland, Ohio: LB Press. White, E. G. *The Great Controversy*. Nampa, Idaho: Pacific Press Publishing Association.


*Websites:*

https://www.christiancinema.com/digital/movie/is-genesis-history

http://www.ldolphin.org/history/pbccd2/pbcCD2/www.pbc.org/dp/catalog/catbybook.html https://www.cai.org/bible-studies

https://www.cai.org/bible-studies/seven-laws-prayer

https://www.biblestudytools.com/commentaries/jamieson-faussetbrown/ https://biblehub.com/library/

https://www.bible-knowledge.com/battle-verses-against-demonic-

attacks/

---

*Movies:*

DeMille, C. B. 1956. *The Ten Commandments.* Motion

Picture Associates.

Stevens, G. C. 1965. *The Greatest Story Ever Told.*

Kershner, I. 1980. *Star Wars: The Empire Strikes Back.*

Davey, B., Gibson, M. C. G. 2004. *The Passion of the Christ.*

Newmarket Films.


*Documentaries:*

Medvedeva, S. S., Rysavy, J. 2015. *Secret of Water: Discover*

*the Language of Life.*